FEARLESSLY CHOSEN

A JOURNEY THROUGH HIS HANDS
TO COMPLETE HEALING

STACEY A. LUCAS

Paperback: 978-1-64746-462-2
Hardback: 978-1-64746-463-9
Ebook: 978-1-64746-464-6

Library of Congress Control Number: 2020916120

Dedication

For my children, Katey and Jacob.
Thank you for the strength you have given me just by being born. You have always been my greatest cheerleaders! God blessed me with the gift of you.

CONTENTS

Introduction vii

SECTION 1—FEAR—GIVING POWER TO
     THE ENEMY. 1

Chapter 1: Who is for Us and Who is Against Us? 3

Chapter 2: Peter Denied Him—Do We? 9

Chapter 3: The Shame of the Woman 18

Chapter 4: The Silence of Spiritual Attack 28

SECTION 2—WHEN WE HAVE FAITH, WE
     TAKE ACTION! 39

Chapter 5: Paul Was Blinded—So Was I 41

Chapter 6: Spirit, Soul, and Body 51

Chapter 7: Healed by the Power of His Hands 64

Chapter 8: Gifts of the Spirit. 78

SECTION 3—FEARLESSLY STEPPING INTO
        THE CALLING. 91

Chapter 9: Brave Like Esther—Following the Call 93

Chapter 10: Stay on the Path. 104

Chapter 11: ME FIRST. 114

Chapter 12: Fearlessly Chosen: Why me? Why Not Me!
        Why Not You?. 125

INTRODUCTION

I stumbled out of the public restroom into the sea of Christmas shoppers at the outside market. A single pinpoint of pain stabbed me in my head! It felt like a stray bullet from the nearby gun show had pierced my brain. I reached up to touch the back of my head, feeling for a bullet hole—no hole. Tears started to well up as my feet carried me deeper into the crowd.

Hot tears streamed down my cheeks, and suddenly the pinpoint of pain exploded around my head like flashing lights. It was like the ascent of thousands of fireworks followed by bright, colorful explosions through my brain! My feet stopped walking, and I tried to assess what was happening. After all, I had worked in the medical field for twenty years. I had a mindset that I would only go to the emergency room if I were on my death bed. So I stood still with my head rupturing and tears still streaming, amongst the crowd of shoppers.

In all my pain and tears, I noticed an older woman suddenly approach and ask me for directions. I forced myself to listen to her words. As I focused on them, on her face, and on her, it helped pull me temporarily from my pain. I was better somehow like the inferno had been turned down. Yet I knew it hadn't left.

This assault on my body was the beginning of a two-year journey of darkness and destruction, the source of which I searched for relentlessly, in a desperate bid for survival. I can't give away what I uncovered at this point; you'll have to be patient. It was a physical onslaught that caused damage to my mind and body that should have killed me. The attack was not only physical, but spiritual, and it racked my soul, trying to destroy me.

* * *

When I thought about writing this book, the first words that came to mind were: *fearless, without fear, bold, and brave.* I was grateful for those words and wrote them down in a place where I could see them daily. As I began to compose sentences and passages, I remembered some words of Mother Teresa that I kept taped in my journal to look at every day. These words gave me courage then, and continue to inspire me today.

She wrote, "Pain and suffering have come into your life, but remember pain, sorrow, suffering is but the kiss of Jesus, a sign that you have come so close to Him that He can kiss you." My first thought was, *why is there pain and suffering, if you are real, Jesus?* What I have learned through this journey is that God does not cause pain and suffering; Satan does.

In today's world, we see sickness everywhere. We all know people who are not feeling well— people who are experiencing many different symptoms, and often their doctors can't find an explanation. Others have diagnoses to explain their physical pain, but they have not received healing.

People are looking for answers, going from doctor to doctor to relieve their pain. I was that person. I was sick, and no one could find the cause. When *nothing could be found,* I felt panicked and worried I was going crazy. Was I really experiencing these things? Was I making it up? Was I looking for attention? Had I brought this upon myself?

This way of thinking was often selfish and fear-based. I had to stop and write out these feelings to help me discover the pattern. The physical illnesses were real, but so was the fear. What I found was that I must make a choice: I must choose to be faithful. As I shifted my mindset, I started to find answers which led me to healing.

However, when I finally overcame my trauma, I was prompted by something that terrified me even more than my healing journey. I was told that I needed to share my story. I stopped dead in my tracks. I felt a hot, heavy wave of shame, guilt, and vulnerability wash over me. I shook at the mere thought of it. Tears poured from my eyes as I was overwhelmed with anxiety.

I was frozen by concern that if I shared my story, I would be ruined; no one would believe me, no one would care, and everyone would laugh and mock me. But then a still small voice whispered. *"I have chosen you."* God wanted me to share it. I knew that if I acted courageously, He would give me the words.

Why was I chosen to experience physical pain and emotional darkness? Was it to teach me to trust God? Why me? This question was at the forefront of my mind nearly every day as I suffered over the next seven years, searching for answers. They came in ways that blessed my life.

One of these answers was the power to understand how to read the scriptures and pray. I know that sounds basic to many, but not to me. This was foundational. I had never understood how to communicate with God; I mostly thought that he didn't care because he knew I was a sinner anyway, so why bother with praying? I needed to know how to connect with God.

I also needed to find answers in the scriptures, and where to even begin reading them. I accepted the challenge to read the Bible, and I completed it in one year, but what did I get out of it? Nothing. No answers, no light, just bits of things every once in a while. For the most part, I was confused and could not understand what the Bible was trying to tell me.

If you feel the same way, let me share with you the answers to this for my life and millions of others. This way of thinking changed my whole understanding: 1) read the New Testament before reading the Old Testament, 2) pray before reading, and 3) understand that Jesus loved to use stories to teach people. With these three key points, I started reading scriptures again. Suddenly I felt that the words on the page were speaking to me. I was finding guidance, answers, and true power from reading His word.

Being filled with this power and light from the word of God, I started to find answers to the big question that plagued me. Why was I chosen to experience the physical pain and emotional darkness? The answer came in Isaiah 43:10. I'm not going to share that here, but I will say this. It was so that I could bring forth His Light! Jesus chose me to show others the healing path that lies in and through Him.

This book is the foundation of my testimony. If you are ready to understand your calling, walk the path, and start the healing journey, read on. I was fearlessly chosen. I had not chosen Him, but He had chosen me just like He has chosen all of you!

SECTION 1

FEAR—GIVING POWER
TO THE ENEMY.

CHAPTER 1
WHO IS FOR US AND WHO IS AGAINST US?

"I know your deeds, that you are neither cold nor hot.
I wish you were either one or the other!
So, because you are lukewarm—neither hot nor cold—
I am about to spit you out of my mouth."
Revelation 3:15-16

Prayer:

God,
It is time to stand firm in my faith and trust in You. I
know that your love for me is enough.
In Jesus' name,
Amen

* * *

Light and Darkness. Sun and Moon. Life and Death. Heaven and Hell. Jesus and Satan. What is this list all about? They are opposites. These are extremes of each other. Yet we know that in the balance of life, opposition is in everything. We spend our lives trying to seek one and not the other or praising the one and fearing the other.

Beep, beep, beep, beep, pulsated the steady rhythm of the medical monitor. Heart rate, blood pressure, and oxygen saturation seemed to all be within normal levels. I looked down at the patient resting free from pain as he slept through another hour, giving his body the critical time it needed to recover and rest. I headed out the door to check on another patient. All was routine but not routine. I understand these machines and have used them in the medical field for over 20 years. I know there is opposition in the world of medicine and healing that can baffle the mind of any medical professional.

When a person's heart stops or breathing stops, he shows all clinical signs of death. When CPR is given, suddenly, the heart seems to almost jumpstart and continues the rhythm of pumping life-saving blood throughout the body. The medical field deals with a form of opposition in all things—life and death—literally.

Another war being waged between the life and death of your spirit affects your heart and your soul. This war has been going on since the beginning of time, even before we came to earth. In Revelations 12 (New International Version), we read:

7 "Then war broke out in heaven. Michael and his angels fought against the dragon, and the dragon and his angels fought back.

8 "But he was not strong enough, and they lost their place in heaven."

9 "The great dragon was hurled down—that ancient serpent called the devil, or Satan, who leads the whole world astray. He was hurled to the earth, and his angels with him."

Even in Heaven, we chose sides and fought. Jesus bet his life on this battle. He wanted us to pick Him and not Satan. Sometimes we are great at choosing the right side. We are filled with light and love and want to please God. Those are good days—great days. But there are also times we fall behind. It seems to happen hour by hour. We wake up on the wrong side of the bed, and we watch the effects of "Murphy's Law" take hold. Every hour can feel like a failure, with Satan winning a day, a week, or even years of our lives.

Just as Satan is fighting hard for us to make mistakes and distance ourselves from God, Jesus is fighting hard to find each one of us individually and help us return to God. Remember the parable of the Lost Sheep in Luke 15? Jesus is out looking for each one of us. He did for me even though I didn't know it.

3 "Then Jesus told them this parable:

4 'Suppose one of you has a hundred sheep and loses one of them. Doesn't he leave the ninety-nine in the open country and go after the lost sheep until he finds it?

5 "And when he finds it, he joyfully puts it on his shoulders

6 "and goes home. Then he calls together his friends and neighbors together and says, 'Rejoice with me. I have found my sheep.'

7 "I tell you that in the same way there will be more rejoicing in heaven over one sinner who repents than over ninety-nine righteous persons who do not need to repent.'"

We all have a journey. We come to earth to choose light or darkness, black or white, God or Satan. It is that clear. However, Satan is subtle. He is good at mixing tiny drops of black into the white, which starts to gray the white, drop by drop. He does it by combining moral truth with small lies. We begin to feel guilty and begin to wonder about the truth we were given. We question things or think we are sinners who can't stay with God. We turn from Him and start to walk slowly down the path in the darkness one step at a time.

There have been many times on my journey when I felt myself walking with my Father, yet I was still living in darkness. We may find ourselves in this place when we have made significant changes in our lives, but we still are in darkness. The despair and yearning for things to come are challenging to endure, and the ability to stand up straight to wait in the Light of God is tough to do.

Waiting. How many of you enjoy waiting for answers when you are talking to someone? We hate it. We want answers now. We expect it now. I did the same thing with God. I expected Him to answer my prayers in the way I desired, but he had a different path for me. I simply had to wait, and that was the hardest part.

During the wait time, Satan sent powerful darkness my way. The power of doubt with its dark inky tentacles slowly and silently glided into the cracks of my mind. He seized upon the opportunity and gently wrapped it around me until I was slowly suffocating. Doubt has that power, and it is easy to fall prey to it.

Then the concept of "second-guessing" reared its ugly head. I thought I was doing okay and felt a particular plan would turn out. Was this the answer to my prayer? I hoped this time would be different. What was wrong with me? Why couldn't I just catch a break in the world? What would happen today? It was a lot of doubt to deal with. *Why even bother praying or planning? The world was going to do its own thing anyway. Why do I even try to start anything? Do I get stopped by everything? Why bother trying? Because each time I do, I find myself not accomplishing what I wanted.*

Have you ever said things like that? They're *blame-focused* and childish, yet easy to succumb to. That way of thinking can be very damaging. A short time ago, I wrote: "The despair is so real at times when I am alone with my thoughts in my time of waiting. I pray for a cure, but it never comes." Those absolute extremes are easy to fall into the habit of saying. Things like *I'll never,* or *it is always,* can deplete your hope and fill you with doubt.

In that doubt, I found myself suddenly flip to this: *God will come. He will bring light to the darkness when it is time.* Then it shifted again to *the waiting in gloom for light to come will never happen.* That was how I saw the extremes—the light and darkness—and I felt them at the same time. I sat and waited in the blackness for sunshine, and it came, spilling over me. I was warmed, but suddenly I felt fear, and the murkiness swallowed me up again. Up and down. Down and up. It was so frustrating.

However, the Lord's light overcame it all for me. I want to show you how. Simply turn and follow Him. I know that simple things are not always easy to do. It is not easy to wait in the darkness for light. It is not easy to go on the ups and downs of life. It is a simple choice to hold to the Lord, but the hard part is hanging on tight as we go through life.

Do you know who is for you and who is against you? Do you know how to recognize it? I hope so because the journey you are about to take will not be black and white. It won't be easy to see the enemy and what he does because he is cunning. He works your mind against you, starting with simple doubts. He waits to see which doubt or negative thought will ring true with you. Once he has dialed into that frequency, he is unrelenting in his cunning way and will fire "all the flaming arrows" at you! (Ephesians 6:16)

Are you ready to continue with me to know how I came to find my Savior? Are you prepared for a journey that breaks rules wherein many people think being saved means to be forgiven as a sinner, and to follow Jesus? If you are, then you are taking a positive step in choosing who is for you and not against you. I came from this experience *Fearlessly Chosen* and have not turned back. Are you ready? Then let's dive in!

CHAPTER 2
PETER DENIED HIM—DO WE?

Galatians 1:10 "Am I now trying to win the approval of human beings, or of God? Or am I trying to please people? If I were still trying to please people, I would not be a servant of Christ."

Prayer:

Now Lord,
I am only concerned about Your word and Your plan; being a people pleaser does not bring peace, but God-pleasing does. I pray, Lord, for guidance to overcome this way, these thoughts of how to make everyone happy, and look to You. You are first; I am second. I want to love as You love, Lord. Everyone and everything else come after that. I can't be a servant of Christ while putting everyone else first!
In Jesus' name,
Amen

* * *

L uke 22: 3-7 and 54-62 (NIV) lays out two compelling stories. One is the story of Judas Iscariot, and the other is that of Peter. Both of these men walked and talked with, listened to, and witnessed miracles of Jesus Christ. They were called, chosen, and asked to leave their professions to follow Christ. As they followed, they found the witness of the truth in all things, and ultimately, they were both apostles of the Lord. The very definition of an apostle is to be a witness of Christ.

Something also interesting to note is that they both had their choices, their agency, to follow Jesus or not to follow Jesus. We have the same opportunity. We read in Matthew 4:

19 "'Come follow me,' Jesus said, 'and I will send you out to fish for people.'

20 "At once they left their nets and followed him."

Peter made a choice to follow right then—no delay. Wow. That is real faith!

Jesus called Judas to be an apostle in Mathew 10:4. He had the choice to follow or not to follow. He followed, as far as we can tell, for a time. I'll share more about this a little later on.

Both of these stories prompt me to ask several questions: Do we deny the Lord, our Savior? What does that look like in our lives? If someone questions whether we are believers, do we also deny it? If someone presents harsh opinions or tries to tell us something that is in opposition to our core beliefs, do we deny Christ to avoid the conflict? If, on social media, our beliefs are challenged, do we stand up, or do we crumble to avoid contention?

Why do we deny Christ? It's simple. We are afraid—we are not exercising faith. Many of us are people pleasers, or we are seeking the approval of man. In Galatians 1:10, it says:

"Am I now trying to win the approval of human beings, or of God? Or am I trying to please people? If I were still trying to please people, I would not be a servant of Christ."

When we fear others, we try to please them so we can be accepted. But if we are following Christ, there will be times when others won't like us and will seek to fight us. This is the time to exercise faith and believe that God will help you.

If we are afraid of mankind and the backlash, we are not demonstrating faith. For me, contention between family members or verbal abuse is what I would suffer if others found out what I experienced. For the longest time, I lived in this fear.

Here is the internal struggle: when we have known Jesus, and we know that He loves us, we can still fear and succumb to peer pressure. We don't want to be called out in front of our friends or family, who may question our beliefs. What if we break? I know I carried fear of what others might think. I denied my Savior for many years of my life.

In Luke 22:54, it says:

"Then seizing him, they led him away and took him into the house of the high priest. Peter followed at a distance."

This scripture caused me to pause, reflect, and freak out a little bit. It kept hitting me over and over again like a question, *why would Peter need to follow at a distance?*

It is easy to guess. He probably wanted to know what was happening to his friend, his Master, but did not want to be caught by the angry mob. Peter knew the danger and still needed to carry on God's will even during this trying time of the Savior. But here is the real question for me. Why did *I* deny Him? Why did *I* follow the Lord, "but at a distance?"

I had gained an enduring, powerful witness of Jesus. I felt Jesus, and I experienced pure light! Yet when people questioned the story and my actions, like selling my house or retiring early from my job, I would say things like, "I wanted to get out of debt and save money," or "I felt it was time to stop working." Many were satisfied with those answers. But it was not the truth. The truth was and is that God told me to leave my job and sell my home. I followed His direction but gave other people different answers than "God told me to."

God chose me to do great work with Him. I was *fearlessly chosen*, and I must follow Him; yet it was easier to avoid the persecution and say, "I wanted to get out of debt. It was time to retire." That was what I was doing. I was following Christ, as Peter did, but at a safe distance.

The persecution doesn't come from strangers, but mostly from those I love and care for. I think it is because they don't understand my experiences, and maybe they don't believe me, but I have to share it. When persecution comes from those you cherish, it can rock your foundation of love and truth. It is easier to be at a safe distance than to be engaged in fights and arguments, and listening to others peck away at what I know to be true. But even though I gave them those lame excuses, I still followed what God told me to do, sold my house, and retired from my job.

Now I am declaring my testimony in this book for all to read. It will be here in print to be considered over time. If you have ever had a witness of God in your life, and you feel called to serve, then you go out and serve.

You've seen Satan throw his fiery arrows at all of us, and he never stops. It says in Ephesians 6:16:

"In addition to all this, take up the shield of faith, with which you can extinguish all the flaming arrows of the evil one."

He never stops, so we need to know that we can be hit and succumb to his temptations, just like Judas Iscariot did. This is important to note. Satan does not attack fully in one swoop. We make choices that open the door to the attacks. His fiery darts never cease, and over time, like acid rain, it weakens and wears us down. Through our bad choices, we are worn to the point of breaking so that when the big temptation happens, we make the horrible choice that allows Satan to get us.

For Judas Iscariot, his plot was foretold by David in Psalm 41:9.

"Even my close friend,
someone I trusted,
one who shared my bread,
has turned against me."

And it was prophesied by Zachariah in chapter 11:

12 "I told them, 'If you think it best, give me my pay; but if not, keep it.' So they paid me thirty pieces of silver.

13 "And the Lord said to me, 'Throw it to the potter'—the handsome price at which they valued me! So I took the thirty pieces of silver and threw them to the potter at the house of the Lord."

This scripture lays out two choices, to either follow Jesus or Satan. Judas was an apostle of the Lord and was with him, watching many of the miracles Jesus performed. We know that he was an agent who functioned like a treasurer and kept track of the money to buy the necessary things Jesus needed.

Here is something fascinating. When Jesus was in the upper room with the apostles, he performed an act of love for his trusted friends, his inner circle, his best friends—He washed their feet. In John 13:5, it says:

"After that, he poured water into a basin and began to wash his disciples' feet, drying them with the towel that was wrapped around him."

But in John 13:2, it says:

"The evening meal was in progress, and the devil had already prompted Judas, the son of Simon Iscariot, to betray Jesus."

Jesus still reached out and washed his feet even though he already knew Judas would betray him. How many chances does the Lord give to us to change our ways? It feels like limitless amounts.

Back in Luke, 22:3, it says:

"Then Satan entered Judas, called Iscariot, one of the Twelve."

Judas was not living his best self. He witnessed the miracles of Jesus, like healings and casting out of demons, but somewhere he still was making choices that were weakening him. The scripture goes on to say:

4 "And Judas went to the chief priests and the officers of the temple guard and discussed with them how he might betray Jesus.

5 "They were delighted and agreed to give him money.

6 "He consented, and watched for an opportunity to hand Jesus over to them when no crowd was present."

Think about it. Judas was with the Savior! But still, Satan never stopped tempting him and trying him. We must take that as a warning that if even an apostle of the Lord can fall, so can we! We must protect ourselves every day by wearing the full armor of God. (See Ephesians 6:10-20).

I want to share with you what I feel is the order of importance of the armor of God. In my opinion, the helmet of salvation is the first fight of defense! The knowledge of your position in God is because of your salvation and redemption in Christ. The helmet of salvation protects your mind. The mind is Satan's chief battleground. If Satan gets into our consciousness, he can wreak havoc to the point that he can destroy not only our life (like Judas) but others as well. Ephesians 6:

14 "Stand firm then, with the belt of truth buckled around your waist, with the breastplate of righteousness in place,

15 "and with your feet fitted with the readiness that comes from the gospel of peace.

16 "In addition to all this, take up the shield of faith, with which you can extinguish all the flaming arrows of the evil one.

17 "Take the helmet of salvation and the sword of the Spirit, which is the word of God."

The girdle, or buckle of truth, represents a clear understanding of God's word. Like a soldier's belt, it holds the rest of the armor in place. "Gird your loins," means to prepare for action. We prepare ourselves to take action in the battle against evil by learning the truth through prayer and scripture study. Buckle up!

The breastplate of righteousness protects vital organs such as our heart and lungs. It also protects our spiritual core. When we accept Jesus into our lives, we become connected with Him. We do all we can to follow Him. Strap on that protection and keep the fiery darts from penetrating your heart!

The shield of faith is an added defense. We should use it to protect ourselves from whatever Satan will throw at us. It takes practice to get into the habit of picking up the shield. It takes faith to believe that it will work for you, and it takes practice to defend yourself from the blows of Satan. If we build our confidence in Jesus and the gospel, then we can make it. The sword of the Spirit is the only offensive weapon we have. With the sword, we can strike back at the enemy. The word of God is a part of this sword. When we use our testimonies and share with others about Jesus Christ and what He has done in our lives, we are mighty against the enemy. However, that means we have to read every day and share it!

Feet fitted with the readiness [shoes] that comes from the gospel of peace. When we are wearing these "shoes," we have goals and direction in our lives. We are also willing to take the gospel to all the world. We are ready to step into the battle against Satan and fight back. But again, this takes practice, hard work, and a commitment not to get lazy. Because if we get lazy or casual, we will be taken down by the fiery darts of the evil one.

That is a lot to do, but if we look back at Peter, he never wasted time. When Jesus asked him to follow Him, he immediately obeyed. He loved Jesus, was with Him and sought to be like Him, even in the time of confusion and trouble. Jesus loved him enough to warn him that he, too, would deny Him (like Judas but not to that extent).

To reflect, we always have choices. Judas had a choice. Peter had a choice. The result of Judas' choice was one that killed him:

"So Judas threw the money into the temple and left. Then he went away and hanged himself." (Matthew 27:5).

For Peter, it was slightly different. In Luke 22: 34, we read:

"Jesus answered, 'I tell you, Peter, before the rooster crows today, you will deny three times that you know me.'"

It was true. Peter did stay at a safe distance, but thankfully it was not for long. He chose to return. Even though it was a bitter moment in his life, Peter learned from that time forward that he could repent. He did not doubt, but felt the light and wanted to be the example he was meant to be.

Remember, it all comes down to choices. Do we choose to protect ourselves with the full armor of God? Do we want to read our scriptures daily? Do we choose to pray to keep our minds and thoughts protected? Do we repent daily so that we can stay close to the Spirit? Do we forgive others as Jesus did? Do we make decisions that lead us to Christ or Satan? Just like Judas and Peter, we all have our choices.

CHAPTER 3
THE SHAME OF THE WOMAN

Prayer:

Heavenly Father,
Each day is a struggle against sin and temptation. Give us the strength to overcome cruelty with grace and hate with love. God, remind us that our actions matter. We do not fight a physical battle but a spiritual one, and with each act of compassion, we build your kingdom. Help us to be Kingdom Builders today.
In Jesus' name,
Amen

* * *

Shame. A painful feeling of humiliation. It can be a mix of regret, self-hate, and even dishonor. To put the background in place for this chapter, let's define the difference between shame and guilt. According to Brené Brown, "Shame is a focus on self. Guilt is a focus on behavior. Shame is, 'I am bad.' Guilt is, 'I did something bad.'"

In John 8:1-11, a woman was brought to Jesus by the scribes and the Pharisees. She had been caught in the act of adultery. The people want to know if Jesus would follow the law and have her stoned right there, or if He would propose something different for her. Time passed, and the group that had gathered tried to guess what Christ would do. Physically, he drew something on the ground with his finger. The tension in the crowd thickened. The Pharisees and scribes discussed whether Jesus would say to cast the stone. After all, she broke a commandment, and justice must be paid.

The scripture goes on to say in John 8:6-8:

> "But Jesus bent down and started to write on the ground with his finger. When they kept on questioning him, he straightened up and said to them, 'Let any one of you who is without sin be the first to throw a stone at her.' Again he stooped down and wrote on the ground."

Jesus, in his loving way, was giving everyone in that crowd—those that loved him, those that hated him, and those that needed him, time to think and evaluate their own problems.

Once the self-assessment happens, we read that "those who heard began to go away one at a time, the older ones first..." The verse concludes with this statement, "...until only Jesus was left, with the woman still standing there." The realization and depth of this story is the fact that we *all* sin. We all mess up. The guilt and shame that fell on many hearts that day can happen to any of us.

Their response to being "caught in something" was a painful feeling. The accusers felt humiliation, regret, self-hate, and dishonor. Ultimately, they were filled with shame. But the Lord can forgive us if we change our ways and follow Him. This story concludes with verses 10 and 11:

"Jesus straightened up and asked her, 'Woman, where are they? Has no one condemned you?' 'No one, sir,' she said. 'Then neither do I condemn you,' Jesus declared. 'Go now and leave your life of sin.'"

The way Jesus told the woman that she was not condemned, that she would not be judged, was full of grace and mercy. The final part of the scripture was a warning. It was to "leave your life of sin." It is that moment in all of our lives that we have to make a choice. Are we going to follow Jesus and do our best to change our ways, or will we succumb to temptation again?

I wonder whether that woman indeed went her way and did not sin again. Did that encounter of love and grace with the Savior change everything for her? It's possible, and I choose to believe she did because shame can arise from past sin to haunt us. However, we can take care of our sin and guilt through Christ—through accepting him, following him, and repenting.

* * *

The hungry, desperate woman sat in a worn wooden pew of the church. The chant of the priest sang out, signaling that the Holy Communion had begun. The incense rose, the Eucharist and chalice were held upward, and the woman sat gently rocking her newborn baby as she watched everyone walk forward to receive Holy Communion. She didn't stand up or step forward because she was ashamed. She was a sinner—not worthy of receiving the bread of life because of the rules. You see, she was pregnant out of wedlock. She was also not married in the church, so she felt it was a double whammy. She seemed to be frozen in the seat, yet a tear slipped down her young cheek and splashed gently on her baby's forehead.

What kind of person was she to sit there in all her shame while everyone else moved on to receive the body of Jesus? That's how I saw myself for many years. I was that hungry woman— desperately, spiritually hungry for His living bread and water.

I lived with that shame for years each time I attended Church. I watched other women who I thought lived the perfect life or had the perfect marriage. I would think, "She has the perfect kids." So I sat still. Alone in my little world, blaming myself for being a sinner. I knew deep down many of the people walking up the aisle were sinners too, but they were allowed to eat; I was ashamed, so I did not go up and partake. I sat, feeling like I had a big scarlet letter "S" on my chest for "sinner." I felt unworthy to sit there—unworthy to receive what was rightfully mine because I looked to people and their rules instead of to God and His mercy. I was so much more of a sinner than the priest who didn't want to baptize my baby. My beautiful child was punished because of me…more shame.

* * *

Now, think back to chapter one and the concept of opposition in all things. What is the opposite of shame? It's pride—not the pride of the world, but in being well-pleased in the things we accomplish, in our self-worth, and in others. When Jesus was baptized Heavenly Father said in Matthew 3:17:

> "And a voice from heaven said, 'This is my Son, whom I love; with him I am well pleased.'"

God was and is pleased with Jesus' baptism. That's all I wanted for my baby. She should not be punished for my sin. I wanted to be loved and accepted by God. But there I sat with my butt glued to the seat. Not allowed for communion, not permitted to have my daughter baptized, and Satan was ready to attack. Satan's go-to message is that of shame. How deeply you feel it is how little you think of yourself.

We are all living with some kind of shame because we all sin. It seems that more women are prone to feeling shame. We can see it across the duration of time. In the Bible, the story I shared was about the woman caught in adultery. What about the woman at the well?

In John 4:7-30, Jesus found the woman at the well. Many of you are familiar with this story, but let me share my perspective. Jesus was a Jew, and Jews stayed away from Samaritans. Yet Christ did not comply with tradition and go around into the Jordan Valley. He walked directly to a well in Samaria, where He met a woman. She knew He was a Jew. She said in verse 9:

> *"You are a Jew, and I am a Samaritan woman. How can you ask me for a drink?"*

She didn't know who he was but still gave him water. Jesus then created an environment that allowed the woman to learn His identity through the Holy Spirit, saying that He was the living water. As the Spirit touched her, she desired this living water as well:

> *15 "The woman said to him, 'Sir, give me this water so that I won't get thirsty and have to keep coming here to draw water.'"*

Jesus now needed to teach her and help her so that she could drink of *His* living water, gain a testimony of Him, and change her sinning ways. He asked her to get her husband.

> *17 "'I have no husband,' she replied. Jesus said to her, 'You are right when you say you have no husband.*

18 The fact is, you have had five husbands, and the man you now have is not your husband. What you have just said is quite true.'

19 'Sir,' the woman said, 'I can see that you are a prophet.'"

Have you ever been called out by God before? I have. I know how painful it is to share this same story of shame as with the woman at the well. I don't have five divorces, but as I am on my third marriage, I have had enough. For the longest time, I felt I could blame getting divorced on my ex-husbands. I thought I would be justified in doing so, and so did friends and family around me. However, as I read this scripture story over and over again, I had an intense feeling that it was my choice. I allowed my actions. I have my faults that contributed to divorce. I carried the blame for my choices and wrote the pain of my first marriage and divorce in a poem.

* * *

BROKEN

Cute hides broken.
Broken is at the bottom of a very thirsty well that can never be filled by the power of alcohol.
Friends are pretty, but cute keeps you safe for a time.

Cute is convenient but never exciting...
Until you add the power of the drink, and your guard goes down.
The drink drowns the pain for a while, but this drink leaves you thirsty for more.

Suddenly your plans, dreams, and future have changed as the ring slides on your finger, and your belly grows.

Soon cries of a baby shatter the calm of the night, and days and nights become a grind.
Words soon fly within the walls of the home that have shattering effects on your emotional state.

Following months and weeks of these words, the power of the drink washes away the pain for a while.

Years roll into each other, and you find your belly expanding again, but the bank account shrinking and poverty growing.
Words beat against your self-worth until you begin to search for a new kind of relief.
There was a night of relief, flirting, fast-paced parties following the heavy drink in the form of white powder.
For three straight days, the land of possibility was at your feet.
Worries faded, and you found a spark of freedom, but at the cost of nearly losing the children.
As the sober crash of those three days hits, the result was ending up alone and more broken than before.

Hearts were broken for children, for adults, because the expectations were shattered.
Thoughts were broken when they turned into spiteful actions.
Words beat the emotional and physical bones of each other when they were said out of hatred and with drink.
Drinking from many different waters never soothed the soul, cut the thirst, or mended the broken.
Being beaten, battered, and broken by words, and no one knew the wounds of the soul but one.
And....
Divorce was the result of the damage, disappointment, and destruction.

Jesus knows all our sins, our secrets, and everything we try to hide, but He is still willing to interact with us who are lowly and fallen. Like I shared in the poem about one of my marriages and divorce, I started out broken going into that marriage and did not find any healing. But I quickly entered into a second marriage and found more heartache and more "broken for my broken."

My shame increased as my second marriage fell into another divorce.

In the scripture, Jesus picked a fallen Samaritan woman doing a very routine chore of drawing water and taught her about living water, changing her ways, and allowing the Spirit to touch her heart. She was a woman and not a Jew. The woman had fallen because of how many husbands she had, and therefore had no respect in any community. She did not have a title, a position, or an education that would give her status. She was not even named in the scripture story; however, the woman at the well had an open heart and mind, to be willing to be taught by Jesus and the Spirit. She saw Jesus as someone who required a drink, so she served him.

She then received the revelation that Jesus was the Messiah:

25 *"The woman said, 'I know that Messiah' (called Christ) 'is coming. When he comes, he will explain everything to us.'*

26 *"Then Jesus declared, 'I, the one speaking to you—I am he.'"*

Think about the significance of this revelation given to a common woman performing a necessary chore. Jesus wants to bless all of us, no matter how flawed we are.

* * *

In her book, *Un-Ashamed,* Heather Davis Nelson says, "The most powerful way to combat shame is to be known and to know others truly. As we share our shame stories or the ways it has tried to silence us—and these stories are met with compassionate empathy—shame fades away. It lessens the fuel of isolation and fear."

How many women look in the mirror every day and are ashamed of what they see? What does that reflection reveal? Too many of us see things that are not there because the veil of shame covers who we are meant to be, holding us back from the life God created for us:

"But whenever anyone turns to the Lord, the veil is taken away." (2 Corinthians 3:16).

We get so comfortable with shame that we use it as an excuse to travel the easy road in life. God created us to do great things, so we need to empower each other to take off that veil and see ourselves for who we truly are, not who we think we are. For example, in Luke 8, we meet a woman who had an issue of blood for twelve years. She had done everything she could to be healed by the physicians, but nothing had worked. Just as I had done for two years.

Think about suffering from and being unclean, uncomfortable, and unloved for twelve years of your life. Many of us feel that way, and we start to listen to Satan, thinking that we are inadequate. But there was something of hope with the woman. When she had heard about Jesus healing all matter of infirmities, she wanted to give it a try. And why not?

She had shame, pain, and felt no love from anyone. She was at the bottom. All she could do was reach upward. She followed him even with a busy and noisy crowd all around thinking if she could "touch the fringe of his garment..." that she would be healed...and immediately, her flow of blood ceased." She did! And she was whole!

Jesus immediately felt that virtue or power had left him. The woman was not hidden by the crowd any longer and was vulnerable. She was exposed on all sides. Jesus then taught a powerful lesson for all of us:

> *48 "Then he said to her, 'Daughter, your faith has healed you. Go in peace.'"*

For anyone who is in shame, please know that the Lord never leaves you. Remember all of my shameful stories: my shame at church, with my marriages, and with my divorces? It is a part of this life, but we can use it as a tool to find ways to heal just like the woman at the well, the woman caught in adultery, and the woman with the issue of blood.

How? By being honest, vulnerable, and willing to follow God. There was a glimmer of hope, a time I supposed Jesus saw through my shame, through all of the layers of sin and hurt, and looked at the real me. Not the person I saw, living with shame and guilt. Jesus died on the cross to save me from sin. Why was I still letting remorse control my life? Why did I let sin that had been forgiven control my life? How could someone who felt unworthy find healing?

She had the faith to do it. That was the secret. Faith! I am not perfect, but I am perfectly me—and I am still loved by Jesus.

CHAPTER 4
THE SILENCE OF SPIRITUAL ATTACK

Prayer:

Heavenly Father,
Spiritual warfare is real. Evil is here around us every day.
But we know that the enemy was defeated at the cross.
He will keep trying to steal, kill, and destroy us. You,
Lord, have provided everything we need to fight the battle.
Lord, I pray for the strength to pick up my armor to fight
against evil forces in every way. Thank you, Jesus, for
never leaving me or forsaking me to fight this on my own.
In Jesus Name,
Amen

* * *

Shopping! Today was one of my favorite days of the year. Christmas shopping was the day that the women in my family came together for a time of laughter, food, and fun. Together with my mom, sister, and daughter, we would spend the day shopping together, walking through booths and booths of Christmas cheer looking for the perfect gifts for family and friends. I have always enjoyed exploring people's creative ideas that have come to life.

That morning I got up and hit the road for the hour drive toward our Christmas shopping adventure. I had my coffee, I was thinking of all the gifts I needed to buy, and I was getting more excited the closer I got. I arrived a few minutes early and parked the car. The lights, colorful banners, the booths bathed in green, red, white, and shimmery tinsel filled my eyes with wonder at the spectacle. The smells of hot cocoa, cinnamon sugar, and other delicious baked goods were the second thing to greet me. I took in a deep breath of the savory and sweet smells, and it opened a floodgate of memories from previous years of attending the festival.

I turned off the engine, took out the key, grabbed my purse, stepped out into the festive air, and locked my car. My eyes begin to feast on the holiday spectacle, even from the parking lot. I walked quickly from my car, and with each step, I got closer and closer to the booths with wooden crafts, handiwork, stuffed bears, and home decor, all the way to the spun sugar cakes; and then it hit! Maybe I shouldn't have drunk all that coffee after all. I refused to say it was my age, opting to say it was the result of having children. Suddenly, I needed to use the restroom.

I made the journey toward the west side of the booths and let my eyes lead the way to a restroom. I knew we would be here for hours, so visiting the restroom now would pay off later. I was definitely ready for my family and the shopping!

As I left the stall and walked to the sinks to wash, I saw many women with excitement and cheer in their eyes. They had all waited for this day just like I had. I reflected in the mirror and watched the mothers, children, sisters, and friends wash and prepare for the best day of shopping!

I pushed through my hand washing routine: two pumps of soap, around and around in the palm, all the while thinking I needed to hurry back out there so that I wouldn't miss the others. While holding onto the cool laminate countertop, I reached up to flash my hand at the sensory on the spout. Instantly the cool water flowed over my hands. Over and over and around my hands, I mechanically went through the motions, my hands slipping past each other as I rinsed the soap from them.

I drew my hands out from the water and waited my turn to tug on the paper towels. Everyone was pulling so many towels; they seemed to be waving away from me. I focused on one and grabbed it. I gently tossed it in the direction of the trash can and walked out of the public restroom into the sea of Christmas shoppers at the outside market.

As I walked, I suddenly felt a stabbing pain from the base of my head that seemed to drill through my entire brain mass, ending at my eyes, which quickly watered, sending tears running down my face. The single pinpoint of agony continued to slice through my head! It felt like a stray bullet from the nearby gun show had pierced my brain. Though the shoppers in their busyness walked all about and around me, I felt utterly alone. I reached up to hold the back of my head and checked for a bullet hole. There wasn't one. Hot tears kept streaming as my feet carried me deeper into the crowd.

Suddenly the origin of my torture burst all around my head like a flash! It was like the ascent of thousands of fireworks, and then colorful lights flashed through my brain. My feet froze in place and I tried to assess what was happening. After all, I had been in the medical field for twenty years. I was trying to work through a logical explanation of this sudden onslaught of such intense pain.

As I tried to work through what it could be, it took all my concentration to stay upright. A stray thought suggested I go to the doctor, but my trained mindset took over. I would only go to the emergency room if I were on my deathbed. Since I was still standing and conscious, I pushed that thought away. I stayed there with my head exploding and tears still streaming, amongst the crowd of shoppers.

The flashes of pain intensified and nearly took me to my knees. Waves of exquisite distress had come on with no warning. I had never been sick like this before. I grabbed the side of a booth to steady myself. *Breathe!* I kept coaching myself, *inhale, exhale, in, out!* After 10 minutes of this pain not budging but only amplifying, I found myself reaching into my purse to get medicine. I thought if I could swallow a few pills, I would be able to fake it through the day. With shaking hands and tears still rolling, I swallowed the pills in hopes of stopping the agony as quickly as possible. I continued to grip the booth for support.

My gut seemed to nudge at me. I wondered when the pain was going to subside. I'm glad that, at the time, I didn't know what the future held. I only knew that at this moment I was helpless. I could barely function. I felt as if this was something more than a migraine, something more sinister, darker. I kept focusing on my breathing as shoppers passed by me.

I got hit with another thought—to call my daughter. My breath caught! Thinking about making a phone call like that was nearly debilitating. I still had to steady myself with one hand on the booth while I fumbled with my phone with the other, breathed, and fought the pain. I slowly swiped the phone and found her contact. A trickle of sweat went down the side of my head and another down my back. The pain intensified.

I punched "call" and waited, sniffling and wiping my nose with my sleeve. Finally, my daughter answered. I blurted in short quick sentences about the pain of the "migraine" I was experiencing. I did my best to pull up all the strength I could to sound confident, so she wouldn't worry. I even tried to make it a bit of a joke by telling her that if she came and found me lying on the ground, at least she'd know what was going on.

The tears didn't stop, and I never released my grip on the booth. I continued to concentrate on breathing as more beads of sweat formed on my forehead. Shoppers still poured past me. I started to feel that I was invisible. Impossibly, the pain gripped me even more! My heart started to beat faster and faster as if to run away from having life squeezed out of it. I was sure the shoppers would be able to hear it thumping as it slammed against my chest wall.

This new heart pain hindered my rhythmic breathing, and I thought I was going to pass out. I realized what I must look like in my mind's eye—a forty-something-year-old woman with tears and sweat running everywhere, holding onto a booth, lost in a sea of shoppers—pathetic. I thought it was ironic to be in such distress, standing in a place full of total strangers, and no one else could see it. They were oblivious to the horrible discomfort, my posture, and my tears as they continued to go about their business.

After nearly 20 minutes of excruciating head and chest pain, a thought popped into my head about my health. Up until this point in my life, I had never had a headache—not once! And suddenly, I got clobbered with one that was nearly debilitating. (I have had hangover headaches before, but never one from being sick). I tried to distract myself by wondering whether I had caused this at all, but thinking about it only increased the agony.

Suddenly, an older woman approached me. Her eyes connected with mine and the crowd of shoppers seemed to fuzz out and fade. She carefully and steadily shuffled toward me.

Even through my pain, I could see details of her hunched back through her Christmas sweater. Her steady gaze and sweet smile helped me stay focused. She laboriously scooted over to me in her matching red sweatpants and black Velcro shoes. The wrinkles in her sweet face and hands gave away her age. She must have been about eighty years old. She gently moved toward me and asked, "Where is the entrance?"

I gasped for a breath of air to stop my head from popping. I forced myself to listen to her words. I focused on them, on her face, on *her* needs. When I shifted from focusing on me and became curious about her needs, the pain left. I was better somehow; it was like the fire in my head and chest had been turned down, and it helped pull me temporarily from the distress. Time slowed during our encounter. I could sense something from her. I felt a sort of comfort and power, or maybe it was energy—like light. The question had been asked, but I still had not given my answer because I was busy leaving my turmoil for a place of hope.

I finally shared the answer she had been seeking, but she never released me from her gaze. The light that came from her eyes was powerful. I was being released from the gipping torment—even if temporarily—and she thanked me. Her gaze emanated light, and I sensed an exchange of love, like she had been sent to me. She was an angel.

I know that sounds crazy, but I believe she was sent as a sign to tell me that I was not alone in this crowd of hundreds—that I was known. She kept me from passing out and falling to the ground. As the shoppers continued their crisscross pattern back and forth, she was lost from sight in the busyness, and I slowly released my grip from the booth. I was better somehow; it was like the searing in both my head and chest had been turned down.

It was whisper-quiet at first. I could hear my name being called. It seemed distant. It came closer and closer until I heard it a little louder. I willed myself to focus on my name, and just as suddenly as my pain had come on, it instantly stopped—just as if water from a faucet had been turned off. It left me in a little state of shock at its sudden absence. The violence in my head and chest had finally ceased. I looked up and saw my mom, sister, and daughter standing in front of me.

My daughter looked a little concerned with my distant stare. I knew she was aware of my pain, but seeing them pulled me back into the moment. They asked me if I was ready. I told them I was. This small conversation also helped pull me further from the sting. My daughter gave me that, *Let's shop till we drop* look and we went about our Christmas festivities.

* * *

On the drive home, all I could think of was how grateful I was that the assault on my body had ceased. I glanced in the rearview mirror at the colorful packages and felt exhausted. As I pulled into the driveway and turned off the car, I thought, *I need to share what happened today with my husband.* I got out of the car, gathered the packages, and headed into the house. My thoughts were racing with worry, in anticipation of how I could explain my experience, and hope he would believe me. After putting the packages down, tucking my treasures away, and getting things settled, I recounted the story.

He seemed to be listening to everything, and as the last word fell from my lips, I knew I needed to go and lay down. I had reached that level of exhaustion where all I could do was rest. I wanted and needed a nap—something I never did. I got up, and with the heaviness of an exhausted body, trudged to the bedroom. I slipped off my shoes, reached for the covers, gently pulled back the soft sheets and blankets, and stiffly tucked my body into the cool warmth of the fresh bed.

Suddenly, like a crack of sound that a solid wood bat makes as it connects with a 90 mile-per-hour baseball, my head was knocked forward off the pillow. I was awake! Then a gripping torment seemed to split my head open. The flashing, twisting pain was back with a vengeance. My head seemed to scream! The sudden movement woke up my husband, and my experience from that afternoon came flooding back. It was happening all over again! All I could do was try to breathe through it as if I were in labor with my children.

Deep breathing in, two, three, four, and out, two, three, four. Focus! In and out. My chest and neck echoed with the thumping of a heart that was running for its life away from that cold evil hand again that wanted to silence it! "Here!" I heard the voice of my husband. I gently cracked one eyelid open just a slit to see him place a glass of water and some headache medicine on the nightstand.

As I lifted the first pill to my mouth, all I could think of was the pain and that swallowing this would help. As the cold water hit my tongue, and I drank, the rushing coolness seemed to distract me from the flashing and popping, but nothing could pull the torment away. I quickly took the second pill and focused again on breathing: in, two, three, four, out, two, three, four. I forced myself to focus on a memory—on how I fought through natural childbirth.

I thought about my work in the medical field and the pain I had seen others endure. Breathe! Breathe! I had to get through this! Ahh, my chest was going to explode! The pull and strain on my heart were too much! I suddenly felt a tugging and tightening against my vocal cords as if that cold, cruel hand reached for my throat to squeeze off my voice from calling out to God to free me!

I tried to speak, but only a whisper escaped my dry lips. I was being choked. I continued to try focusing on breathing, yet the other half of me seemed to be wrestling with something. It was becoming a full-on battle in my head, my heart, and my throat! Like a wounded soldier, I wouldn't give up but tried to fight back. After about 20 minutes of this war raging inside me, I felt the effect of the medicine quietly take over, and I slipped back into a deep and dreamless sleep.

In the morning, I felt myself rise upward, almost being lifted from the depth of sleep and into the waking morning as I gently opened my eyes. I looked about the room; all was well. I carefully sat up in bed and felt the back of my head. No bumps, no pain, I felt my heart, steady, slow, and calm; the only hint that anything had physically happened was the whispering voice, but the rest of it was gone. It was Sunday. That was it! It was over.

As I started going about my business of the day doing routine work in the kitchen, I was suddenly struck again. I felt the bullet-like blast enter through the back of my head. I was caught off guard and taken aback by this third attack, and I was starting to be concerned that maybe I had an aneurysm, I was having an active heart attack, or I had a brain tumor. There was an intense smell and a terrible odor as well. Those thoughts consumed me, but they did not move me to go to the hospital. Again, after about 20 minutes of head flashing, heart twisting, throat squeezing, eye dimming, and profuse sweating, it left.

* * *

Monday morning was a workday. I woke up, and as my eyes connected with daylight, the left side of the back of my head rebelled again. As I rose to get out of bed, I had to hold the back of my head simply to try to speak. My voice was weak. When I tried to talk, all that came out was a whisper. The tears flowed once again, but this time my heart was racing differently. I thought it was going to come out of my chest. After about 20 minutes, the head pain subsided, but my voice was still weak, and my heart did not slow down!

I broke down and decided to call a doctor with whom I had previously worked to see if he could see me. He was a neurosurgeon. I thought that if anyone could figure this out, it would be him. The scheduler gave me an appointment for the next day to have an MRI (magnetic resonance imaging) and an MRA (magnetic resonance angiography).

After the pain subsided, I got dressed and went to work. I know, I know, all of you reading this are thinking that I am crazy. As I'm writing this, *I* think it's crazy, but that is how stubborn I was. Going to work that day, still thinking I was ok, I started the routine of what I do best, taking care of people. I pushed and pushed and got through my day. My head started pounding again. I couldn't speak above a whisper, and my heart raced. I knew that something had happened. It had been three full days of this. Three days! I finally decided to go to the emergency room to have a CT (computerized tomography) scan and see what was happening.

The emergency doctor couldn't believe how fast my heart was racing and that I was just now getting to the hospital. The numbers I saw on the screen even frightened me. Just to help give you some medical perspective, a normal resting heart rate is 60-70 beats per minute (bpm). Fast and abnormal for a resting heart rate is 100 bpm and over. When exercising, a heart rate for my age can be in the range of 88-149 bpm, with the MAXIMUM being 175 bpm.

My heart rate was over 110 at rest! The ER doctor ordered injections to slow my heart rate and to relieve the pain in my head. After doing test after test that were each negative, the ER doctor wanted to send me to another hospital for more examination, such as a lumbar puncture (spinal tap). I refused this option (more pain!) and told him I was seeing a specialist the next day.

The medication administered through the injections had worked: no more headache, my voice was returning to normal, my heart rate had gone down, and I was feeling better. All of the boxes were checked, so I left. I did not want to be told that *it was all in my head.* I did not want to have the medical community treat me like I was stuck in a vicious cycle that would never provide answers to physical tests. I feared that I would be told *nothing was wrong with me.* I dreaded having pain like this for the rest of my life and never receiving an answer or diagnosis to explain what was happening physically. My fear was coming true.

The testing done during my first ER visit concluded precisely what I feared. All the testing came back negative—*all of it.* I knew I was aging; I was in my mid-forties. But I had never understood what being sick felt like, much less being ill and no one finding the answers. Something had happened to me. I could physically testify to the pain. It had come and gone with such intensity that it was *not* a fluke event. All three times I was convinced I would find some kind of tumor or aneurysm.

As I left the ER with no answers, a flutter of fear filled my gut. My husband drove the car, and I looked out the window, watching the grey, chilly sky offering no answers either. Mile after mile, the grey fog seemed to engulf the car and symbolically, my life. I had started down this road of *no answers and more pain,* and there was no color, no light, and no end in sight.

As we drove, my thoughts became more clouded and anxious. Maybe this was my punishment for all the wrong choices I'd made in my life. Maybe everything I had learned in church was right. Perhaps this was my fate as a marked sinner—to have no answers and struggle daily through pain—my punishment not worthy of healing, only worthy of suffering.

And yet, as the last mile rolled beneath us, I knew I *could* do one thing. I knew I could pray. I might not be worthy of being healed, but I felt that I could at least pray to ask for a diagnosis. Again, I thought that I was not esteemed enough to pray for healing. As a sinner, I only hoped I deserved some explanation. This desire for answers started me on a two-year journey of doing just that. I wanted at least that much.

SECTION 2

WHEN WE HAVE FAITH, WE TAKE ACTION!

CHAPTER 5
PAUL WAS BLINDED—SO WAS I

Prayer:

Lord Jesus,
Open the eyes of my heart to see what You need me to see,
my ears to hear what You need me to hear, my mind to
know what You need me to know, and my heart to love
who You need me to love.
In Jesus' name, I pray,
Amen

* * *

I have shared my story, scriptures, and prayers that helped me through an incredibly challenging time. But honestly, when I was attacked on that December day, I did not start suddenly attending church, reading scripture, or finding my relationship with Jesus. I simply did the bare minimum and only prayed to get a diagnosis.

All of the scriptures and strengthening of my testimony started after my healing. Sin and knowing that I was a sinner, damned by progression toward any salvation, kept me stuck.

Yet the pain kept me motivated to try to find answers. The story of Paul helped; he was someone with whom I identified. Paul didn't ask people for their approval. He was tested and prepared ahead of time for his experience. He was made qualified by God, by the Spirit, and by the faith, and we can be made whole too!

I was lost just as he was. Outwardly, Paul was part of a group of people who tried to catch everyone else breaking the law. He was fighting against God. I was, too, mostly. I was fighting the very God by judging myself, in the same way that Paul was judging others. He was blind to what God could give him, and I was blind to the blessings God was prepared to provide for me.

I appeared to be okay. I had a great job, a home, and a great family. But inwardly, I was blind to the actual relationship I could have with Jesus. I was stumbling around feeling for answers to help explain my physical pain and sickness, when internally, spiritually, I was in a dark place. I did what I could to numb the shame with alcohol. Unfortunately, drinking added to my inability to see the real help I needed because I was so focused on what I didn't have.

As a forty-five-year-old woman, I was not living my best life; I had already lived through the devastation of two divorces and can honestly say I was not making sound decisions. Living with the shame that goes along with one divorce is hard enough. But after two, you start thinking it is you that is failing. You are the one that is not doing enough, and the one that is mad at God because you have to blame someone for your pain. The question that racked my brain over and over again was, *why was everyone else living happily ever after?* I thought I would never have that. Day after day, the hopelessness slowly crept in until I knew nothing else. With feelings of despair, failure, and shame pounding at me daily, I did what many people do. I numbed my life even more with alcohol.

At 14, I had started drinking alcohol, experimenting, seeing what it was all about, and wondering what my limit was. It was easy to drink with friends, and most of that started on the weekend. I didn't drink every day, but if I started drinking, I would never know when to stop. The power of my buffer seemed to numb my senses to everything—especially my ability to make good decisions. Following terrible choices, I found myself left in a mess. Because I was in the mess that I had created by my poor choices, alcohol seemed to feed that shame I needed to numb again, and so the cycle continued.

After the first divorce, I drank more regularly. Then following my second divorce, I drank even more deeply—the depth of this drinking was extended and left me with episodes of blacking out.

* * *

DROWNING

As I sat in my car looking out at the frosted windows, I noticed a cloud of steam filling the vehicle with each exiting breath. I cracked the top of another beer. This was my second beer; I was drinking again, and the depth of this drinking binge was painful. My daughter was getting married. I took six long swallows. The pain was rising again. I let out a breath of air as the thought ran through my head, *you don't have enough money to help with your own daughter's wedding—pathetic!*

The image in my head of my ex-husband with his girlfriend standing beside him, handing over the check to pay for our daughter's wedding, seemed to be stuck on repeat. It seemed that with each replay, I drank another can. I could not get the image, the emotion, or the words of that day to stop.

I snapped open a fifth can and chugged it down, trying to scrub that image out of my head, trying to wash away the guilt and pain. My mind suddenly snapped! A picture of the wedding day came into my mind. I saw the bridesmaids and the groomsmen dressed in their best lined up, ready to start the processional. I saw my daughter arm in arm with her father. As I looked over to see who I was with, I saw nothing, just space— empty, like a black hole.

I flashed myself back to the present. I lifted my seventh beer, toasted to the air, and washed away the last of the anguish. With each swallow, I felt myself sink into the false welcoming darkness. The numbness was complete—I blacked out.

* * *

Consistently making poor choices, listening to my shame, and drinking, broke my spirit. My soul was broken, and my *broken* was even broken. I became the exact person the devil is prowling around looking to destroy. He will prey on that shame, as he did me. He will get into your thoughts until you believe everything he is telling you. Then he will throw in all the worst memories. You will see every bad thing you have done or that has happened to you. He will later claim that *it's your fault!*

At that point, you lose all control of your thoughts, your dreams, and your health. You pray, but the devil is already there. He had been in my life for years because of the poor choices that I had been making. Like Paul, I didn't know the feeling of God or Jesus. I didn't think they could provide true blessings.

Even before Paul was Paul, he was Saul. In Acts 21:39, we learn that he was born in a Greek city in Cilicia. In Romans, 11:1 we discover that he was a Jew from the lineage of Benjamin, and in Acts 23:6, we know that he was a Pharisee, so he knew the laws and traditions of Moses and prided himself in that knowledge. However, he did not use the codes to draw himself closer to God. He spent his time judging others and going after people who were breaking the very letter of the law.

We are first introduced to Saul in chapter 7 of Acts verses 58-59. Stephan was being persecuted for declaring that he saw God the Father and Jesus. He would not deny his testimony and was stoned for it. Saul was there at the stoning as witnesses laid their garments at his feet, but he never threw a stone.

Watching Stephan be stoned after listening to his testimony of witnessing God the Father and Jesus Christ did nothing to change Saul's heart. In fact, following this experience in Acts 8:

1 *"On that day a great persecution broke out against the church in Jerusalem, and all except the apostles were scattered throughout Judea and Samaria.*

3 *"But Saul began to destroy the church. Going from house after house, he dragged off both men and women and put them in prison."*

He was doing what he was best at—judging others and catching people in their "sin," then punishing them for following Christ.

When we are not following God and even throwing out our faith in Christ, thinking the law itself has the power to save or condemn us, how do we expect to receive blessings? Are we lost and fallen forever? I mean, how can God love us, who are fallen? How can He still love anyone who is fighting against Him? How could He love someone who was making awful, sinful choices? How can God love people who are even leading brothers and sisters into more sinful ways? How can He love a person like Saul, who was persecuting others for their beliefs?

In Acts 9, we see what happened to Saul:

1 *"Meanwhile, Saul was still breathing out murderous threats against the Lord's disciples. He went to the high priest*

2 and asked him for letters to the synagogues in Damascus, so that if he found any there who belonged to the Way, whether men or women, he might take them as prisoners to Jerusalem."

Saul was in the very act of getting more of the letters with the names of Christians who were following Jesus. He rode out to get them, bind them, and put them in jail.

Have you ever been so focused on a task, a job, or part of your life that you are blind to anything else? You are determined to do this work no matter what, and you don't even stop to think that something or someone else could get in your righteous way?

3 "As he neared Damascus on his journey, suddenly a light from heaven flashed around him."

Saul's attention was suddenly and directly diverted from his purpose to looking around him at what was happening! He was bathed in light, stopped in his tracks, and told to pay attention to this.

4 "He fell to the ground and heard a voice say to him, 'Saul, Saul, why do you persecute me?'"

Whose voice was that? Who was calling him out? Saul had the same question:

5 'Who are you, Lord?' 'I am Jesus, whom you are persecuting,' he replied."

What would you do if you had that experience in your life? Would it get your attention? Would you change?

I think it is interesting that, even in the crowd, the people who were with Saul were also able to hear the voice, but they saw no one. Everyone who was with him heard something.

7 "The men traveling with Saul stood there speechless; they heard the sound but did not see anyone."

I understand this feeling. I, too, have heard Jesus. I also was blind to having a relationship with Jesus because of my choices. I "heard the sound but did not see anyone." When it happened to me, I could not understand what I heard because I did not see it.

Jesus then told Saul:

6 "Now get up and go into the city, and you will be told what you must do."

He had a choice to make. He had been in the act of judging and persecuting others for years. People knew him for this, and he was feared in many cities. Saul was not going to change or waver from his duty, and yet,

8 "Saul got up from the ground, but when he opened his eyes, he could see nothing. So, they led him by the hand into Damascus."

Saul was still headed to Damascus, but his journey had changed. The scripture says that his eyes were opened; he could see nothing. He was blind! He had experienced and had seen Jesus! He heard the voice of Jesus! And yet, he was now blind. Nothing on earth could physically distract him from what God had told him. He felt driven to go to Damascus unlike ever before, but this time not to persecute others. This time not on his agenda. This time to be healed.

I think about Saul on his journey to Damascus, and how in a split second, his life was forever changed. As I neared the place I met my family on that Christmas shopping day, little did I know that my life was going to change forever as suddenly as Saul's did.

When I was spiritually attacked during that shopping day, the evil spirit knew my weaknesses and put all the physical pain I could possibly experience into my head and heart. I was not possessed by the evil spirit that attacked me, but it was a physical fight. This struggle was symbolic in many ways. The pain in my head and heart blocked me from knowing that I could ask for healing.

I was blind to the power of Jesus. I had to find the real reason for the pain in my head, my body jerking about, the night sweats, intense body odor, random blindness, my teeth breaking off, and my unexplained racing heart that would continue to plague me for two full years. I felt compelled in my mind and spirit to find a diagnosis because I did not feel worthy of being healed. I didn't *know* I could ask for that in my prayers—again, more of my blindness.

When Saul's name was changed to Paul, and he was blind for three days, I wonder what he was thinking? Did he feel worthy of being healed? Did he know that Jesus would be the one to heal him? When Paul opened his eyes, did he see what the Lord was telling him, or was he still seeing the darkness of his unbelief? Did he instantly come to know the Lord, or was that in the three days before his healing?

I believe that in those three days, Paul had a change of heart. I think that he reviewed the choices in his life and repented for them, then chose. The Lord called him to do a great work, but he was not quite prepared for it. He had been someone who persecuted the church and fought against Jesus. He had a lot of changes to go through but was only given three days to do it. You see, I was also blinded in knowing what God wanted me to do in my life. I didn't know how to follow Him.

* * *

I was born and raised Catholic. Growing up, I went to church on Sundays and religion classes on Wednesdays. I believed in

God and Jesus, but I did not have a *relationship* with them in any way. I was following the letter of the law but did not *feel* it. They were out there somewhere, but they felt abstract and not a real part of me because I didn't know you could have a relationship with God and Jesus. I didn't know about the Holy Spirit except that he was part of "the Father, Son, and Holy Spirit."

I did not have a good relationship with the Catholic church. After all, I was broken. I hid behind a veil of shame, and I struggled because the church did not help a sinner like me. They were very good at "marking" a sinner, however. I had sinned; there's no denying that. I was pregnant at 18 years old and not married, let alone in the church. I had broken some significant rules. The priest made sure that I felt guilty. I guess to me, it felt like the priest was kind of like Saul. He needed to teach me a lesson because I screwed up. No repentance, no baptism for my child, and no holy communion. Check, check, and check.

I thought the church was a place where I could find Jesus—that I could find a way to repent for the sins I had committed and be made whole again. However, all I felt was that I had a mark placed upon me. The most devastating part was that I thought I was the only sinner in the church and that somehow everyone else was free from sin.

My shame said to me, *why is everyone else receiving the holy communion, and I have to sit in the pew as they all walk by?* That stuck with me my whole life. I felt I was only allowed to *look* at the way towards Jesus, but I could not *participate in* the Church to *know Jesus* or to build a relationship with Him.

Despite that, there was one thing I continued to do. I continued to pray throughout my life. It was something I felt driven to do. It was sound reasoning and logic, but there was also a deep need for it. However, my heart *never* knew that I could intimately *know* Jesus. This was part of my blindness.

After all, I was a sinner, and so I was going to be on the outside forever.

When the evil spirit attacked me that December day, it *knew* this weakness of mine—that I thought I could never really know Jesus. Yes, I could pray, and that was good, but because I was a sinner, there was still doubt that I could ever be well again. The evil spirit worked with that doubt and continued to fill me with hopelessness. In that state, would I ever accept Him as my Savior, as someone who loved me, and someone who would heal me? I only felt worthy of trying to find a diagnosis, not recovering. I continued to be blind to the knowledge that I could enjoy a full relationship with Jesus. I was like Saul—blinded by sin from the very thing I needed most of all, Jesus.

CHAPTER 6
SPIRIT, SOUL, AND BODY

Prayer:

Heavenly Father,
You say that our body, soul, and spirit must be kept
blameless at the coming of our Lord Jesus Christ. I pray
for my body to be free of any illness that is holding me
captive. I pray for my soul to be healed of any shame,
guilt, or fear that is keeping me from You. I pray for my
spirit to be filled with living water so I can know pure joy.
Thank you, Lord, for showing me the way to complete
healing.
In Jesus' name,
Amen

* * *

How do you build a relationship with Jesus? How do any of us do it? The better question for me at that time was, a*m I worthy of a relationship with Him?* I didn't even know I could do that. Because of my lack of know-how to build this relationship with Christ, combined with my poor choices, I was left open and vulnerable for a spiritual attack.

Now before you think the spiritual attack happened overnight, it didn't. The darkness seemed to roll in like a fog, hovering over me, waiting to settle into all of my parts that were vulnerable. It was slow, dark, and heavy, pulling me to drift away from the straight and narrow path. That separation presented itself in many different ways. The gulf was from Satan.

The devil is cunning. Most of the time, he *tries* to lead us ever so carefully down to hell. We may not even be aware this is happening. Many people are Christian, but the devil uses them for his purpose. Satan is that wolf in sheep's clothing, carefully leading the flock into danger, and the sheep are unaware of how they are being led and driving others to slaughter.

Satan knew what tools to use on me. Since the mind— our thoughts are the primary way Satan tries to gain access to people, he will hurt their mind and body. I was not aware that the attack was about to happen when it did. The darkness crept in and took over my thoughts, my body, and my soul. It even tried to cloud my spirit because I did not know Jesus as my Savior.

On that shopping day, physical pain hit me all at once, but I had slowly been opening myself up to Satan because my guard was down, allowing him to wedge closer to my spirit. My physical life consisted of working daily with pain, looking for answers, taking more tests, and receiving only negative results. To push down the pain, I fell into more and more drinking on the weekends. I drank to escape, to numb, and to be part of the party.

Following my drinking blackouts, I would wake up and not be able to remember the night, my family, or friends, and then my bizarre pain would be amplified yet again! Each time I let my guard down, Satan got a little more of a foothold.

I would spend time trying to find answers to the physical pain only to be told, "I am sorry. All the tests are negative. We don't know what is wrong with you." The whole painful process started over again, week after week.

I wandered through a valley of darkness with no hope of ever finding the light. Many people, friends, and even my own family did not understand that I was sick and started casting their doubt my way as well. That doubt made me begin to think I was going crazy and that I would have to live this way forever. But I am stubborn. I would not give up altogether. If I was only worth finding a diagnosis, then that was what I would do.

* * *

As the old year of 2013 rolled over into 2014, I determined that this would be the year I found peace and relief. This journey of pain and suffering had started in December of 2012, and following a year of no answers, exquisite pain, and frustration, I knew that this year I could find the diagnosis. I must! I needed a medical reason why all of this was happening.

January 8, 2014 dawned like any other workday. Up, dress, grab my coffee, pray for the pain to stop, and drive to work through traffic. At work, the same routine fell into place—check charts (fight the headache), welcome patients into rooms (hold back waves of pain), take vital signs and per-form physical assessments (breathe through my racing heart), and keep paperwork organized (sweat profusely). However, on this day, something more intense happened than during my previous 13 months of illness.

After getting ready for the next patient, my heart's pump-thump, pump-thump, pump-thump started its famil-iar racing. This was something I was used to. After all, five different doctors said they couldn't find anything to help me. So, I just dealt with it.

However, the pump-thump, pump-thump, pump-thump of my heart raced! Then I felt a new sensation—a constriction of pain across my chest that made me catch my breath and quickly find a chair. I was between patients, so I grabbed the pulse oximeter and slipped it onto my finger. The number that bounced up made me laugh out loud, but then I swallowed hard. 236? What? 236 beats per minute?

My mind raced to my medical training. Resting heart rate is 60-100 beats per minute. Exercise heart rate for my age is about 150-175. I looked again, 236? I'm sitting down! I haven't done any exercise. The hard pounding of my heart, the tightness in my chest, and my voice restricted to a whisper triggered me to seek help.

I got up and went back to talk to the nurse. I told myself this was different, and the numbers scared me. I found her in the staff room. "Can you check something for me?" I asked.

"Sure," she said.

"What does that number say to you?"

The nurse looked at the pulse oximeter and gasped when she saw the number.

Her eyes locked with mine, and she immediately instructed me to perform vagal maneuvers (holding my nose and mouth and trying to blow air out, coughing, gagging, and hugging my chest to my knees) to slow my heart rate down. These interventions didn't work, so she sent word to have the doctor come back immediately.

With no success in response to the maneuvers and the doctor called, she hooked me up to the EKG machine to see if I was having a heart attack. While I was attached to the device, the physician walked in. He looked at the pulse oximeter and the EKG. The machines captured the racing of my heart, and their worried faces caused me to remember my New Year's resolution. This was it! I was going to find the diagnosis. They're at work. I was going to have an answer! He scanned and scanned the results and wrote something down.

This was it! Here it came! "Stacey, you are not having a heart attack, but you need to go to the hospital—immediately!"
My face fell. The pain tightened. Wait. What?
"No!" came my response. "No! I can't go." The doctor and nurse looked at me, confused. "No!" I shouted this time.
"The doctors are going to perform the same sets of tests that they have for 13 months only to tell me they can't find anything, and I will go home with the same heart racing, head pain, night sweats with the intense body odor, the random body jerks, feeling like I have blind spots, feeling like I'm attached to an IV with adrenaline pumping through me! No!" Their faces showed sympathy but also confusion. They didn't understand me, but I simply couldn't put myself through one more diagnosis of "there is nothing wrong with you!"
Finally, after about an hour and more maneuvers with nothing working, he said, "You have to go to the hospital by ambulance, or I am taking you!" My heart seemed to jump, and the bottom of my stomach fell. I was defeated. I knew he was right, that I couldn't keep this up. My heart rate was still at 230 bpm, and I could feel it wearing out.
I called my husband, and he picked me up at work. As he drove through the traffic, I couldn't think. I couldn't feel emotion. I just felt like dying. By the time we arrived at the hospital, I was close to passing out. The nurses and doctors were there waiting for me. The pulse oximeter read 212 (a bit lower, but I had sustained 230 for over an hour). It was crazy how fast they had my shirt off and hooked me up to everything needed to save my life. It was a flurry of activity: oxygen, shots of adenosine and verapamil, a sinus massage, and a carotid artery pressure treatment. Before I knew it, my heart was back to normal.
As the excitement died down, the emergency over, the doctor looked at me and said, "Stacey, you have a condition called supraventricular tachycardia." My eyes did a double blink.

"Wait, you have a diagnosis for me?"

"Yes, you have supraventricular tachycardia. There is a simple procedure we can do called catheter ablation. We will insert a catheter into an artery or vein in your leg and guide it up to your heart. There, the surgeon will record the electrical impulses to find out where the problem is. Once they know, they will zero in on it and use an electrode to zap the area with cold or with heat."

I could hardly believe what was happening. I prayed for 13 months for an answer, and I got one! I finally had a diagnosis. January 8, 2014 was an incredible day for me. My life was finally going to change!

* * *

I felt like a miracle that was about to happen. I was going to have a one-hour surgery that would heal my body. I thought that every symptom I had been suffering from was going to end with this surgery. I had a diagnosis, and would finally have relief! My body, spirit, and soul could finally be free from the pain. That was all I could focus on—to be free from months and months of misery. It was going to be gone.

When waiting for a solution to a stressful situation (like in my case with the surgery), time drags! Finally, it was the day of surgery. Thinking that it was the end of my journey, I was ready. The doctor came in to explain things to me. It would be a routine surgery, in and out in one hour, with a high success rate. I had no concerns about going in, so my mom and daughter went back out to the waiting room with no worries.

However, when I woke up and noticed it was four hours later, I asked the nurse if the time was correct. She said yes but that she didn't know why it took so long. Her eyes were distant, not focusing on me. I was just one more patient to "get through" till her shift ended. I could see her eyes worn with worry, and figured that she was on autopilot with me.

Following this type of surgery, the required procedure was to lay flat for several hours afterward. The nurse was making adjustments in the bed for me to settle in, and in her avoidance of any real connection, she was unaware that she gave me a pillow with someone else's blood on it. I felt that I was a number on a chart and that I was going to have to recover on my own. She was not in a position to be there for me.

As the monitors beeped and tracked my heart, blood oxygen levels, and blood pressure, I lay there without information from the surgeon. My mind hoped for answers, for that wash of peace that should have come over me. The confirmation that my pain-filled journey was indeed over—that tonight, my healing would begin.

As soon as I thought I could be healed, there was a new pain, sciatic pain that ran down my left leg and seemed to burn its memory into me. Fear shot through me, and I caught my breath thinking, *no, this is the pain from the surgery; they did surgery on my leg. This is not permanent pain but recovery pain. Yes, that was it,* I thought again. *It was recovery pain.*

The surgeon entered my room. He looked just as worn as the nurse—as if he had been through a more significant mental battle than merely a physical surgery. It was as if the craziness I was experiencing somehow leaked out of me and spilled onto my nurse and surgeon.

He said that my surgery was more complicated than he had anticipated, but he was confident he had fixed the problem. I was going to stay overnight for postoperative observation, and then I could return to regular activity. With that, he wrote something on my chart, handed it to the nurse, and looked at me with a well-worn half-smile, turned, and left my recovery room.

That was it. I would have to endure the night with leg pain. As the hours slowly ticked by during my overnight observation, there were times that my heart would start on its racing journey again. It would sound the alarms, but it never reached those dangerous levels of 236 beats per minute. I guessed it was fixed.

* * *

On my follow-up appointment a few days later, the surgeon didn't have any explanation for my rapid heart rate now and wanted to put me on meds. I was not prepared for that news because I thought the whole purpose of the surgery was so that I didn't have to have any medication. I was acutely disappointed and started seeking answers in copies of my operative report. I found only added questions instead of the root of the problem.

Years later, I learned from the surgeon that during the procedure, my heart was beating over 200 bpm. My operation note says, "In any event, this was a very long, challenging case, very difficult; it was very long, and so I did not pursue any further ablation for potential tachycardia at this time." All I could think of was that the evil entity did not want to leave its comfort zone, so it went into spasm, beating, racing, and jumping around like a wild fish—trying to stay out of the grasp of my skilled surgeon.

Everything about this was challenging. I had been having tachycardia, night sweats, body jerks, headaches, broken teeth, extreme fear, adrenaline rushes, loss of eyesight, and leg swelling, but not once did any of the dozens of tests show anything but this one. I thought I finally had answers.

* * *

I feel impressed to give you a timeline to help you understand my journey of pursuing the medical diagnosis:

12/08/12 - Sudden onset of headache at the Christmas shopping day.
12/10/12 - First trip to the local ER after a full day of work.

12/12/12 - Eye doctor appointment. I could not see; then I was able to see; I would have split vision, blurriness, blind spots, and darkness, and then my sight would be restored.

01/28/13 - Neurology appointment for the pain in my head, night sweats, random body jerks, and a racing heart.

08/23/13 - Hospital in Tennessee for my racing heart, night sweats, head pain, exhaustion, and more blindness.

01/08/14 - Resting heart rate while at work was 230 bpm. I went to another hospital ER; Resting heart rate was 212 bpm and, finally, a diagnosis of supraventricular tachycardia.

01/16/14 - Heart surgery with complications.

03/30/14 - Mayo Clinic first time.

04/10/14 - Family doctor referred me to Mayo again.

07/30/14 - Mayo Clinic a second time.

Before moving on, I have been talking about finding relief from my physical pain. Something more had to happen, but what? To this point, I had only considered healing with traditional medicine. Yet, something important to understand is the difference between spirit, soul, and body to appreciate my journey.

According to the book, The Triumphant Church, Kenneth E Hagin writes, "Physical oppression can be a direct result of an evil spirit afflicting a person's body." Hagin says that since man has a spirit, he has a soul. The spirit lives in the body, and together they create the soul. Demons can affect and influence man in his body, his mind, his will, and his thoughts, yet not be present in his spirit.

Evil spirits can exert a certain amount of influence as they seek to oppress humankind. They can afflict anyone, even Christians, if they allow it. Of course, evil spirits have their most extensive range of influence if they can embody a human because they can express themselves in the natural realm. Sickness and disease are a part of our mortal experience, and Satan can use it as a tool to damage us.

Sometimes there can even be the real presence of a demon in a person's body that creates sickness and disease. Your body is the house in which your spirit resides. The spirit of man is on the inside while the body houses it. If you are born again, the spirit can't have a devil in it. But your body—the house of your spirit—can have an evil spirit afflicting it.

I had to search for my worth, my self-value. This work helped me understand it more than anything had before. If I had given up and not listened, the evil spirit could have quickly taken complete control of me. I might have allowed it because I felt marked, like I was a sinner, and not loved for who I was.

When we feel we are beyond reach or help, darkness settles in, taking over the souls of believers, because the night of doubt begins to reign. Doubt is destructive, for it depletes all belief, plunging one into hopelessness. Without hope, there is no light. With no light, evil seeks to destroy the Kingdom of God.

A note to all those who are abused: Abuse is a dark place of confusion and despair. Even after people are physically rescued, there is a deep healing that the spirit, body, and soul must go through to be saved. I shall not live in darkness as long as I bear the light of Jesus. My purpose is to lead others out of darkness, doubt, and confusion, and back into the light of His love.

I have helped women who are in this place. They feel worthless and unlovable. In this fragile and empty place, Satan tries to convince them they are useless and will never be valued.

The harsh environment of sexual abuse, child abuse, violence, and sex trafficking, imposed on those who are vulnerable and physically being destroyed, is pure evil. Yet, victims can be rescued. They are of great value. Once they have been physically liberated, a deeper trap may be evident that holds them captive. I feel called to help women out of that abyss. I must shine my light to stop Satan from ultimately gaining power over them. There is a way. We have the edge over him because we have the light of Christ within each one of us. If you are experiencing sudden unexplained sickness, thoughts you have never had before, absent love for God, depression, or little joy, you are under spiritual attack!

When Christ's light healed me and filled my spirit, body, and soul, I knew the privilege and honor of being blessed with the presence of Jesus far outweighed everything I experienced. I was no longer in peril. I experienced both worlds, and the light far exceeded the darkness. So many people are choosing to stay in uncertainty, not realizing how beautiful clarity is.

We all see and experience darkness differently. But it comes from the same source no matter what kind of distress you are experiencing. The devil is here to destroy you and God's kingdom. That is what he spends all day trying to do.

The thing about spiritual attack is that when it happened to me, I did not know that it was even possible. I had never heard of it happening like this—not at church, or at any time in the 20 years I was in the medical field. I believed in spirits, or ghosts, but only as people who came back from the dead to haunt. I was not even sure what all that meant. When I learned that I was attacked by an evil entity, even though I had never heard of it or understood what it meant, I knew it to be true because of the voice and the vision I experienced.

The Holy Spirit was already working on me. There were so many times all I could say was, "I didn't know that was possible." I want people to know many of us have gone through a spiritual attack. I share this story so that you won't have to spend as long as I did trying to figure it out.

In 2 Corinthians 7:1 it says:

"Therefore, since we have these promises, dear friends, let us purify ourselves from everything that contaminates body and spirit, perfecting holiness out of reverence for God."

There is a way to protect yourself from these attacks. You can put on the full armor of God and fight the battle for your life. I have not only survived a brutal assault of the devil, but I now thrive. He has no power over you against your will, so start taking your life back.

If it weren't for receiving the gifts of the Holy Spirit when I was healed, I would not be where I am now. I would not have pursued my healing and believed I had seen Jesus. Those things could not be explained away. 1 Corinthians 16 says:

13 "Be on your guard; stand firm in the faith, be courageous; be strong.

14 "Do everything in love."

My passion is to help people see and escape the darkness. Spiritual oppression in sex trafficking is pervasive. People need to know it is not their fault, the devil can be defeated, and they can be set free from bondage, through Jesus Christ. It will not be easy, but it will be worth it. Women, we must rise up and stand together to help others. We must stop the ease of enslavement and stop being complacent.

"You women who are so complacent,
rise up and listen to me;
you daughters who feel secure,
hear what I have to say!" (Isaiah 32:9)

We have a responsibility to keep our fellow brothers and sisters in Christ. See Philippians 1:12. *Now I want you to know, brothers and sisters, that what has happened to me has actually served to advance the gospel.* Thinking about how to keep your body, spirit, and soul prepared is vital. Your life here on Earth is to help others. May you find that service. I know I did, and my life is filled with peace because of it.

CHAPTER 7
HEALED BY THE POWER
OF HIS HANDS

Prayer:

Jesus,
Thank you for your healing hands, for reaching down and
healing me in body, soul, and spirit. You are the great
healer in the darkest of times. We praise you for all that is
seen and unseen. You are always working on our behalf,
never leaving us or forsaking us. All things are possible
through You. I praise you and give you the glory.
In your mighty name, I pray,
Amen

* * *

THE DOCTOR

Doctor, doctor, doctor
Doctor…Head pain—sharp like a bullet entering
the bone at the back of my skull.

Reaching up to feel if there would be bone fragments and sticky-wet blood, but nothing.

As my hand touched the place of pain, suddenly firework-like explosions, light flashing, brain-twisting, pressure building, blasting through the soft flesh of my brain.

Doctor—see the doctor!

Doctor, doctor, doctor
Doctor....

Find relief! But go to work—the pressure is on me to do it all... pressure to find answers.

Pressure to provide. Pressure, pressure, pressure.

Breathe in two, three, four, and out—suddenly a tightening across my throat that would squeeze across my larynx.

Voiceless! No.... words.

Doctor, doctor, doctor,
Doctor....

Black, dark, 1 o'clock am.... Wet, wet, sweaty wet!

Rise from bed in dripping stink toxic body smells looking at the mattress—a pool of wet sweat stains. Warm water, soap, and scrub, repeat, the scrubbing, get to toxic stench off.

Toweling off. Smelling my skin, the stink is gone until it will return!

Doctor, doctor, doctor,
Doctor....

Random. Random. Left-right! Pulled. Jerked. Working, jerk eyes of patience flash at the movement.

Kick the cabinet at home. Left leg jerks out while driving. I pull on the wheel to the right, snapping the car back into place.

Breathe... focus. Control your legs—JERK! No control, no answer from the brain to the leg.

The leg is on its own. Random...random...random

Doctor, doctor, doctor,
Doctor....
Time for lunch. Cut into the red/green skin of the apple sinking into the white flesh with my teeth and chomp down crunching on the sweet goodness.
Gritty, breaking bite. What?
Why is the apple gritty?
Then the metal taste of.... blood...broken piece of 5 teeth. Random? No!

Doctor, doctor, doctor,
Doctor....
Thump-bump. Thump-bump.... Thump-bump......
Thump-bump....... Thump-bump. Faster! 89
Steady.... breathe! Steady! Thump-bump...Thump-bump.
Thump-bump. Faster! 137
Pressure—Thump-bump. Thump-bump. Thump-bump.
Thump-bump. Thump-bump. Faster! 189
Tightening Thump-bump. Thump-bump. Thump-bump.
Thump-bump. -Thump-bump! Faster! 236!
236!
236!
An icy cold hand feels like it is squeezing, twisting my heart, and the pressure...
Thump-bump. Thump-bump. Thump-bump.
Thump-bump. Thump-bump. Thump-bump. Thump-bump.
Thump-bump. Thump-bump. It, Thump-bump, never, Thump-bump, stops!

Doctor, doctor, doctor,
Doctor....
Blue curtains. Hospital gown. Hairnet. Beeping of machines. Bright lights. Many voices.
Surgery day, tachycardia! Cold washing of the skin on my forearm. The cold needle going in.

A warm flow sinks me from the conscious for one-hour of surgical sleep.

1 hour...

2 hours...

3 hours...

4 hours...

Lightening, burning irritation of sciatic nerve pain. Holding a pillow with another's blood on it.

My heart feels the same; I have no answers. But now I have more medicine! No change, no real change.

Doctor, doctor, doctor,

Doctor....

Tachycardia, night sweats, body jerks, headaches, teeth breaking, extreme fear, adrenaline rushes, loss of eyesight, and leg swelling. I cannot find the answer here with my doctors, doctors, doctors......

Until no more doctors.

Have you ever crossed paths with someone and known deep in your gut that it was not a chance meeting? As if God was personally directing your life—like he was a director in the movie called "Your Life"? What makes a great story or a great movie? Is it watching the main character go through a journey exhausting themselves trying to find the right way, the correct path, the best answers, and having a wise person direct them toward solutions that will take them on a journey to find the truth?

Jesus sent an amazing woman into my life who began preparing me to trust methods other than traditional medicine. She planted the seeds for my healing.

* * *

I felt hope after meeting my friend. I knew that she was a God-fearing woman, and I trusted her on my journey of seeking out alternative methods for relief from the pain. God knew I had done everything in my power, and with doctors to find answers, and nothing was happening. After my last trip to the Mayo Clinic, I needed to do something different. I could not live another minute with my long list of symptoms that were controlling my life.

I needed to find answers. My friend who loves God, trusts Him, and is a Christian, felt prompted to help me seek these answers. I knew that I needed to find relief through alternative methods. I knew that I was not going to live that way anymore.

I was directed through a matter of different circumstances to Lori, a friend of my hairdresser. Our conversation during my hair appointment was beautiful and full of answers. I know God opened her mouth so I could find the pathway to a new direction I did not know was there. Solutions come in many ways, and for me, the clue from my hairdresser was to connect with Lori.

* * *

THE VOICE, THE VISION, AND THE VISITATION

The Voice

In John 16, it says:

> 12 *"I have much more to say to you, more than you can now bear.*
>
> 13 *"But when he, the Spirit of truth, comes, he will guide you into all the truth. He will not speak on his own; he will speak only what he hears, and he will tell you what is yet to come.*
>
> 14 *"He will glorify me because it is from me that he will receive what he will make known to you.*

15 *"All that belongs to the Father is mine. That is why I said the Spirit will receive from me what he will make known to you."*

As I was lying on the table in a relaxed Reiki position, Lori was guiding her hands at my head, allowing the universal energy to flow gently, and I felt peace. Reiki is pain-free and is a way to think through and connect your body, mind, and spirit. Peace, beautiful peace. As soon as I began to feel peaceful, I also began to feel intense pain in my head and my racing heart.

I breathed in and out, and as I did, I tried to focus on the energy. I prompted myself to stay in the moment, to work through the pain—breathe, deep in, two, three, four, five, six, expanding, filling the last space of my lungs with air. The pain grabbed at me again. *I can breathe through it*, I thought. I looked inside myself with my eyes closed, looking for the pain to work through. I continued to breathe in deeper and deeper, trying to cleanse away the pain.

During this cleansing, I began to pray in my heart for help to chase out the pain. I've always tried to pray during my breathing, hoping to be heard. *Oh, God! Please find this pain and work it out of me. You guided me here. You guided me to try these methods. This suffering is exhausting. Please, help me!*

As I exhaled and closed my prayer, I heard at that exact moment a distinct *Voice,* soft, and firm. The Voice became clearer and brighter until it penetrated my bones. My breath caught in my throat. *"Great things will come from this,"* the Voice said. My body held on to the words as they seemed to penetrate deep in my bones. I thought in my head, *what do you mean "great things will come from this?" I am sick. How can this be good, much less great?* But I was filled with such peace, love, and awe! The beauty of the Voice surrounded me.

When I rolled over, it continued, *"This isn't just about you anymore."* Those words seemed to fill my belly and heart—my whole being. They appeared to trigger every emotion that was deep within my body. It was a release of over two years' worth of pain and exhaustion. The only way to express it was through my steady, cleansing tears filled with all the feelings that I couldn't say.

Jesus began to flow in the emotion of it all. *How, Lord, how? I don't understand,* I thought. Again, the Voice repeated, "*Great things will come from this. This isn't just about you anymore.*" I was stunned. I thought, *what do you mean? I am the sick one! Who else can this be about?* No response. Just a feeling of peace, so I was still.

I didn't move, but for my breathing. My mind started to race, from what was spoken to me, to so many questions. How? When? Why? I sought out the Voice again, but I heard it no more. The penetration of the Voice of God left an impression deep within me. That impression became my drive to search for more answers, and those answers continued in the form of more alternative treatments.

* * *

The Vision

My body was on the firm, yet comfortable table. Jessica's voice was calm and reassuring; I could feel her goodness and light. This was the right place, and I knew that deep inside. Her voice began to guide me into deep thought as I prepared for the acupuncture treatment.

As the first hair-like needle gently pierced my skin, I felt a hot spark of pain. I did not vocally disclose the sensation. I had never received acupuncture, so I didn't know what to expect. I thought, *I don't think it is supposed to feel like this. No one ever warned me that it was a painful procedure. But I feel like I'm getting electrocuted in that area!*

I was on my back, and I needed to keep breathing through the pain. Breath in, in, in—in a deep fill-the-belly-through-my-ribs kind of a deep breath. In slowly with meaning, and blow the pain away. Again, I repeated that with each puncture of the different needles. However, the hot sparks of pain pierced all over my body, and it didn't leave. I added prayer to my intervention. I needed relief! I continued to breathe and pray, lying there as hot tears slid out of the corners of my face and down into my ears.

I felt the room become brighter as gently as the sun rises in the east; the room with each passing second became filled with warm white light! It seemed to surround me softly. I was the only one aware of this beautiful light.

Suddenly, in that light, I saw Jesus! His brightness, energy, and power surrounded him. His wounded hand reached and grasped my right hand. I felt comfort begin to enter into me and enfold me. I was caught up in this love, and His voice stilled the pain. It all vanished! I was filled with profound peace.

I looked at him and felt His words. He asked me to turn and look. More people were here in the room with me. I drew my gaze from the face of my Savior to see Mary, the Mother of Jesus, holding my right foot. She was there looking at me, loving me, and encouraging me. I felt her say to look on, and I did.

I saw Michael, the Archangel, at my left foot, filling me with strength. He was also glowing and bright, but not as brilliantly as was Jesus. As I turned to see who was at my left hand, I saw my grandmother, my "Mammaw Pig," gently stroking my hand and smiling at me. My family. One who loved me. One who cared for me. One who was always there for me.

The love and energy surrounded me with white light like a peace-filled cocoon. It was all-consuming and encompassing.

I looked back toward my right and witnessed Jesus, my Savior, speak to me with His eyes. I felt the power of His words gently permeate my heart as He repeated, "*Great things will come from this. It is not about you anymore.*" I was overwhelmed with love and could not deny Him. My understanding was that Mary, Michael, and Mammaw Pig were here to confirm this. Mary was there to support me woman to woman. Michael was there to stand alongside me to keep fighting this battle. My grandma, Mammaw Pig, was the prayer warrior, providing me strength.

Tears of love replaced the pain, and cleansing released the evil I had felt for two years. There was no time signature in this vision. It was God's time—the moment of love and power that stopped the minutes from ticking away. As I took in the glorious visit, I knew that soon this Vision would close.

As my loved one, Mammaw Pig, departed, followed by Mary, then Michael, the Savior looked intently at me again. With no more pain to distract me, his piercing eye reminded me that I had work to do, that this was my first big step in the right direction. His eternal light rose with Him as He began to leave. As He continued to ascend, I felt more peace come into my heart, grounding me to my duty and calling.

Jessica's voice was the next thing I noticed in the room. The needles no longer carried searing pain, and the treatment was over. The Vision had closed. I was still filled with peace, as well as urgency for my mission. I had been chosen to serve God—me, a sinner, and by the world's standards, *a nobody*.

How did this happen? I'm just little Stacey! Why me? All those questions would be answered later, but for now, I knew that with all the living breath I have in my body, I *had seen* Jesus! I knew it! I knew that God knew it, and I would never deny it. I had been encompassed by his peace and His love. I knew I was loved. I was His! This experience was one more seed planted, preparing me for one more event.

Following the Vision that happened during my first visit, Jessica seemed to have collapsed in a chair and appeared utterly worn out. We looked at each other. She held my gaze deeply and shared with me what she had felt during the treatment.

She knew something that she was afraid to disclose to me. "Stacey," she began, "I have to tell you something." I looked at her, and in my heart, I had no worries, no stress, and no fear. I gave her a reassuring look back, and all she could say was, "An evil entity has attacked you."

My head registered those words as they were confirmed in my heart. I knew it. It was as if time stood still, and my mind went to the day nearly two years earlier when I was Christmas shopping. I suffered all this pain because of the oppression of an evil spirit, a demon that caused sickness and disease.

I knew instantly—in a flash—that all the illness, leg jerks, arm jerks, pain, heart sweats, blindness, and headaches had been from the evil one. It was confirmed, and I feared nothing! I also knew, as Jessica knew, that I needed further treatment. She took an active part in helping me seek more care. She knew her skills and ability were not sufficient to help me further. She directed me to someone else, who was the final piece in my physical healing.

* * *

The Visitation

Not long after that amazing experience with Jessica, I found myself once again guided to another caregiver. Jessica had told me that this was not something she knew how to handle. She sent me to an acupuncturist who had a gift of healing along with the gift of placing needles into precise areas of the body. She recommended me to Richard.

The day I arrived at his office, I felt calm, and yet, I had a running conversation in my head about what was going to happen at this appointment. I pulled on the glass door of the building, which led to a small waiting room. There were a few people in the room, and I searched for that open spot that was not too close to other clients.

As I sat in the room, I felt myself start to have the physical symptoms again. My head began to pound with pain, and my heart raced, thundering deep in my chest. I tried to cover up the pain and quickly chose a chair next to a 15-year-old boy. As I sat, I could feel a sense of foreboding and anxiety, also coming from my teenage neighbor. It was as if sitting next to him intensified my pain—like he was channeling what he was feeling toward me. I sensed another woman in the room with an illness she had apparently been suffering over the years, contributing to the accumulation of all our afflictions together.

I wanted to flee, to run, to get out right then. I had never been so overwhelmed by so many different feelings of doubt, darkness, and misery before. It was as if I was picking up on everyone's despair, and it was amplifying my experience. Suddenly my mind remembered what Jessica had said, that an evil entity had attacked me, and I could almost feel the evil that was also coming from the youngster directly toward me. For the first time, my mind was consciously aware of my ability to pick up on this. I wanted to jump up and leave, but I held on, trying to breathe through it.

When Richard came out to call me back to his office, I was happy to get out of the waiting room where I had experienced such a bombardment of despair. My feet quickly carried me into the office, and the intense sensation immediately lifted as I crossed the threshold of his treatment room and sat down. My heart stopped racing, and the pain in my head eased. I knew things would be different this time.

As Richard sat down across from me, I suddenly felt a deep movement from within my belly like a jerk and pull, and I could feel a spark of anger arise. I was so shocked by this that I could barely comprehend the first words out of his mouth. I looked at him across the desk with a flicker of anger that flashed as he held my eyes and said, "I guess we are going to get to know each other very well." I had no idea how true that would be.

Again, I could feel something move about within me. I felt another, more insistent hot rush of fury, and I wanted to lash out! The strength of my emotion was unlike anything I had ever felt before. I needed to glare at Richard, to yell and scream. I pushed the rage away as best I could, but I felt almost helpless at its insistence.

Richard asked me a question in a soft, vibrant tone of voice. "Are you a Christian?" The anger smoldered to red hot, and I had to fight to say the word, "Yes!" I felt the jerking discontent bump around inside me as soon as I had declared it. Richard looked at me intently and continued, this time with the statement, "You will need all the faith and trust in God you have today."

As my ears captured those words, they seemed to penetrate my heart, and the flash of anger was instantly stilled. It was as if God had cast out the hatred by my response to Richard's question. I sat quietly and did all I could to muster up my faith!

Lying on the table, I had a feeling that this was going to be different than before. Richard walked past me and opened the window. I'm was not sure why I noted that at the time, but I knew it was the right thing to do.

I fell into prayer as the first needle sank deep into my skin, carrying with it an electrical shock! My heart, light, and faith began to waver with the depth of a new version of pain. I tried to reach and grasp onto my hope. The electrical intensity of the needles made me cry out, and I could hardly breathe through the pain as my body began to tremble and shake. The table seemed to be thundering underneath my jerking body. I did not think I could endure it.

Richard's resonant voice gave me a bit of strength, but my shaking continued. I tried to go inward to find my light, energy, and faith. I started to coach myself to grasp the imagery of being on an island looking across the water to people I knew and loved on the shoreline. They were calling out, trying to encourage me, but I could not distinguish their words. I could not feel comfort from them.

As he placed each needle, it felt to my flesh like a hot knife. I could not stand one more piercing. My shaking, cries for help, and anguish was at its peak! I cried out inwardly in prayer, "Jesus, I can't do it another minute! Please help me!"

Just as I cried out, the room began to glow by degree, warm, white, and brighter than the sun. It gently captured and surrounded me as the light touching my pain vanished. I opened my eyes in the most intense brilliance I had ever seen, through two pierced hands.

The light flowed through those hands into my eyes, which directed it through my body to my spirit. I felt, for the first time, a centered, cleansing peace, repairing and healing through the warmth. The sensation surged through my head toward my heart, and I felt warmth spilling from it, slowing my thundering heartbeat to normal.

I gazed into the light coming from the scarred hands and felt more love than I ever had in my life. The feeling raced through more parts of my body. It headed to my glands. It seemed to chase the final dark and demonic toxins from the cavities of my body out through the pores of my skin. The evil was flushed out!

I was encircled by more radiance and joy than I had ever experienced. Jesus was standing there with beautiful golden streams coming from both his hands. He called me by name. "Stacey, breathe in the light!"

So that is what I did. I concentrated only on His resplendence, pulling it in through the crown of my head. I sensed it traveling through all the bones, muscles, and everywhere the pain had been, healing it all. In its place was complete peace, love, and warmth. It was beautiful, like all despair was released and replaced with Jesus Himself. I was worthy of Him, of His visit, of being healed, and of His love.

Finally, the entrenched entity in my belly was captured and thrown from my body. Beauty and harmony replaced the violence, filling the cavity of my abdomen with healing. I looked at Jesus. He was smiling at me with love and joy.

As the last particle of light left my body, the warmth and peace remained. I was free.

"I was brought back to the state of great rest and peace without sickness of the body or terrors of the mind." (Julian of Norwich). I was physically healed. It was immediate and final. The peace was complete, and the sickness was gone. But most importantly, the constant feeling of unrest was taken from me in that instant.

* * *

I began to register Richard's quiet, soft voice in my ears. My face was still wet as tears streamed down from all that I had experienced. Richard removed the needles and looked me in the eyes. He told me something I was not expecting. He said that during the session, he saw a shadow leave me and leap out the window.

Everything made sense. The demon was gone. Jesus had cast it out. He healed me! I was free! I had seen, breathed in, and become light. I had seen my Savior, my Lord, Jesus. I did not have to worry anymore. My physical body was free from the pain, and I had been chosen by Christ to follow Him.

CHAPTER 8
GIFTS OF THE SPIRIT

Prayer:

Heavenly Father,
Thank you for filling me with your Spirit. You knew how
my life would be when you formed me in my mother's
womb. You blessed me with gifts to walk in your light and
serve in Your mighty name. You knew what I needed
when I needed it, and I am forever grateful.
Lord, I will honor you and bring glory to Your name,
Amen

* * *

Poem:

Light.
The power and energy that flows from the intensity
glow that fell from His hands surrounded me.
Warmth. The light was gentle, soft, yet powerful to
enter inside me as He directed me to allow the power
to flow within me.

Light.
Warmth, energy; my cells were awakened from their darkened and shriveled state of death and pain to that of filling with power and being healed, and the light touched each cell in my body.

Light.
There was no time, for it was swallowed up in the light of His healing hands.
The hands that blessed the lives of thousands as He walked the earth.

Light.
The hands that cast out the physical disease of the leper, the cripple, the palsy, the issue of blood, were here with power and light casting out the deepest darkness of a demon. They were at my head telling me to "breathe in the light!"

Light.
The gentle yet intense brightness was there to cleanse me and not destroy me! It was brighter than the sun!

Light.
The cleansing, healing, effective power flowed and flowed through my body and chased the darkness, chased the pain, cast out the smell, stopped the jerking, ended the racing, strengthened my teeth, and replaced the years of confusion of no answers. All of that was cast from me—I was free!

Light.
The flow was within each cell, seemingly to resurrect it from depression, hopelessness, even near death, to deep overwhelming joy! The true joy of being freed

from the captivity of the demon! To be replaced with the LOVE, the Light, the healing power of Jesus is that of a miracle.

Light.
This was cast on me. Jesus healed me. Jesus found me. Jesus heard my cry. Jesus came and spoke truth to my soul, and my light from within was given power.

Light.
From this power came an awakening to the gifts that He had given me. My eyes, my ears, my nose, my thoughts, and my body suddenly FELT the power of these gifts.

Light.
The power of discernment, of revelation, of prophecy, of visions, of hearing voices, of mercy and of healing were awakened, and so was my journey into a new calling.

Light.
Through the cleansing and healing power, Jesus chose me. And yet, my journey into this new world was just about to begin.

* * *

Peace and beauty stayed with me, and I was in this light for about two weeks. The expression of love and freedom I felt after two years of physical pain was sheer joy and elation. Little old me, little Stacey was healed by the power of Christ, and I was free, or so I thought.

One morning I was suddenly hit with a slight pain. I thought about it, shook it off, and rolled over in my bed. As I did that, I could smell the odor begin to rise from the sheets, the mattress, my skin, my hair! The smell was back. I suddenly sat up, and as I did the thump, thump, thump, thump, thump, thump of my heart started to rattle against my ribs, and my throat was restricted again! It was happening all over again! NO! I had been healed!

My husband could smell it, as well. I was so embarrassed, and now everything—the light I had experienced seemed to dim by degrees until it was replaced, yet again, by darkness. I felt lost and depressed, and then thoughts began to flood my mind, drowning out all hope. Feelings of immorality, jealousy, hate, and buried rage had returned.

I was crying and aimless as I struggled through the days, trying to fight through work to provide for us. All the peace that I had was gone. I replayed and searched back in my head about the conversation Richard had with me on the day of my healing. What had he asked me to do? He had counseled me to get my head into the scriptures—to surround and protect myself with studying the words of the Savior, to be filled with His strength and power daily. He counseled me to begin reading the New Testament.

As I recalled that thought, my mind was filled again with a flood of negative emotions—jealousy, hate, and anger, and bam! My heart started to race again. I left work and went home to try to think clearly about a few things. I knew that something had to be different. What could I do? I decided to make another appointment with Jessica.

At the appointment, the cycle of angst started again. I had to breathe through it. It was as if I had never been healed! The pain was overwhelming! The darkness, the crazy voices, and thoughts that would not stop were trying to destroy my peace again. I prayed and prayed for the pain to end, for healing power and light to return—to save me! Suddenly, the darkness left me, and the pain subsided. Jessica was there holding my hands, and I felt whole again. She said that the demon had been cast out.

Two. Wait! Two? What had happened? How did I have two? Or did the first one return? My mind went to a flashback, searching my life to know what had gone wrong. The long story cut short was that Jesus had healed me. He asked me to immerse myself in the Word of God, to stay on His path, and to "come, follow Him."

What had I done? I had begun to live in that light, but I had not started reading the protective power of the Word. I had left myself vulnerable again because I had not started reading the scriptures! I immediately left the office and knew where I needed to begin. As I immersed myself in study, I learned more about what I had experienced. The answer was in Matthew 12:43-45.

43 "When an impure spirit comes out of a person, it goes through arid places seeking rest and does not find it.

44 "Then it says, 'I will return to the house I left.' When it arrives, it finds the house unoccupied, swept clean and put in order.

45 "Then it goes and takes with it seven other spirits more wicked than itself, and they go in and live there. And the final condition of that person is worse than the first. That is how it will be with this wicked generation."

I remember crying, praying, and repenting, asking for sincere forgiveness! I could not believe that I had forgotten the power of healing through His light! I could not believe how I had opened myself back up to that darkness again! I vowed right there to cast it all out. As I pulled up to my home, I ran right in and pulled my dusty Bible off the shelf. It cracked as I opened it. I sat and stared at the first passage. It was time to stop running, stop fearing, and start doing.

* * *

I wish I could tell you that the power of the Word of God instantly started to fill my heart and my soul with God's power and love, but it didn't. It took a while. This was not going to come quickly; however, one thing I can testify is that even though I thought I was not getting much out of reading the Bible, I was protected because of my obedience. I could feel that Jesus was pleased that I was choosing Him; after all, He had chosen me.

There was something very humbling and empowering to know that I was chosen to do "a great work," even though I was like an infant at the beginning of this journey. I knew that if I stayed true and faithful, I would be shown what to do with the gifts of the Spirit that were awakened in me. 1 Corinthians 12:

> 8 "To one there is given through the Spirit a message of wisdom, to another a message of knowledge by means of the same Spirit,
>
> 9 "to another faith by the same Spirit, to another, gifts of healing by that one Spirit,
>
> 10 "to another, miraculous powers, to another prophecy, to another distinguishing between spirits, to another speaking in different kinds of tongues, and to still another the interpretation of tongues."

For me, the gifts I was blessed with were that of discernment, revelation, prophecy, visions, mercy, and healing.

My prayers, scripture study, and journaling never seemed to cease. These practical exercises with my "baby spirituality" were helping me to gain insight. It took one year to go through the scriptures, and I didn't fully understand them, but I had obeyed and was blessed. Once I added church and Bible study groups to my life, my understanding began to widen, and my love for the Word started to grow as well. I could feel that Jesus was pleased with my devotion and worship. I was getting to know Him more and more.

There was a story that I came across in the scriptures that gave me hope. I almost missed it completely. In Mark 16:9, it says:

> "*When Jesus rose early on the first day of the week, he appeared first to Mary Magdalene, out of whom he had driven seven demons.*"

I thought, wait, seven? Seven demons? There was a cross-reference to the same story in Luke, and it says:

> *1 "After this, Jesus traveled about from one town and village to another, proclaiming the good news of the kingdom of God. The Twelve were with him,*
>
> *2 "and also some women who had been cured of evil spirits and diseases: Mary (called Magdalene) from whom seven demons had come out;"*

Again, I thought, *seven!* My world seemed to stop as I sat with the Word and in fervent prayer. I seemed to feel a sense of love and kinship toward Mary. I knew what it was like to live with one, and then what it was like to be attacked again because I was not faithfully keeping my side of the promise. I wondered what the experience was like for her.

Again, I felt an overwhelming sense of love toward Mary. My heart cried out with anguish for her. How miserable must her life have been! I can imagine the confusion, physical pain, and fear she suffered. Then, like the light that happened in my life, Jesus found and healed her. Through healing like that, there is a powerful relationship formed. There is a bond of love and loyalty that is unlike any other.

Jesus and Mary were close. He cured her of seven demons. Mary was walking the earth with seven demons, and He healed her at once. Her life radically changed at that instant. I read and reread those simple passages of scripture and knew the feeling of that healing! When I was healed, I was also blessed to develop mercy, discernment, the gift of healing, and much more.

Because I was receiving those gifts, I felt Mary must have received those gifts also. It helps me to understand her total devotion to her Savior—why she was there at his death and resurrection, through all of it. She had that passion for him because of the delivery from her affliction. She had all-encompassing love. For the first time, my connection to the scriptures filled me with light and love. I knew that as I continued to read, I would be led to my next step.

* * *

Because of that, I had more visions, revelations, and comfort with the Spirit. My prayers never ceased. I received understanding, and with it, I was prompted to start my journey toward baptism. I used the gifts of the Spirit to direct me to this decision.

As I reflect on my baptism, I am amazed at the things God arranged just for me to be baptized. It all started by reading a book. The book was a story about someone's journey and experience with seeing Jesus. I was so drawn to the narration and love that flowed from the pages that I rapidly consumed it. At the end of the book, there was a list of charities that provided mission opportunities to do service and help others.

I had never been on a mission trip before or thought about going on one. But at that time, I felt a presence with me pushing me to click one link. That simple motion sent a ripple out into the universe that opened a way for me to make my journey to a foreign country. Before I knew what was happening, I was on my way to Africa with a bunch of people I had never met before.

The week before my trip, I kept hearing God say, "You are going to get baptized while you are in Africa." I felt my heart skip, and doubt started to fill my mind. As silly as it sounds, I immediately started arguing with God, saying, *why do I need to get baptized? I was baptized when I was a baby.*

Being raised Catholic, I did not understand the whole concept of being baptized as an adult. The idea of committing to follow Jesus was exciting, and yet I was a little fearful—what if I continued to make mistakes? However, the thought that comforted me was that I would be closer to Jesus than ever before.

Now, there was only one slight challenge. That was the fact that baptism is in water. As a healthcare provider for over 20 years, I know the germs and dangerous microbes that unclean water can carry. I know the cost it can be to your digestive system. I knew this would be a huge hurdle to cross to be baptized in Africa. My fear was ***getting in that water***! If there was one thing the organizers of the mission trip hammered into us was to STAY AWAY from the WATER! However, God persisted with the promise that I would get baptized in Africa.

Upon arrival in Africa, the part of the continent we were on happened to be in its rainy season. This is that BIG type of rain. The kind where it lasts for weeks and weeks. On one day we were going to work at our village. The bridge was washed out, so we had to go to another settlement closer to our hotel. Working in Africa and helping others brought joy into my life, and it prepared me to step closer and closer to Jesus.

I would feel the heat of the day, the work we were called to do, the lives we were blessing, and I would feel such a love for the little children and for the women. I was changing, and suddenly my story of all I had been through was brought to my remembrance. Yet I did not share it with anyone, except for one.

She and I had discussed some things about baptism. We had shared, I guess you could say, the "logic" of baptism, but not the spiritual aspects of it. Our work continued until one afternoon the sun finally came out after days of rain. The celebration of the sun's return was noted with rejoicing. I was in awe at all the people here we were so grateful for.

With the return of the sun, our trip leader suggested that we go see the Indian Ocean. My heart seemed to leap and jump. I felt something coming with this trip. Could this be the time for my baptism? I was not sure, but I knew it would happen in Africa.

As our bus edged closer to the ocean, I saw it stretch outward endlessly to the horizon. It was beautiful—unlike any water I had seen in the U.S. before. The water seemed starkly white to me instead of blue or green. We all emptied the bus and felt a pull to go toward the sea.

As I stood by myself, a man came up to me and said I would be baptized in the ocean today. I think I was in a mild state of shock. To this day, I don't know how he knew what I had been told about being baptized. I had not shared that story with him. God was the one telling me about the baptism, and now others were prompted with it.

So here I was, in front of a bunch of people I had only met a couple of days before sharing with them how God had told me a week before that I was going to be baptized. The power and gentleness of this touched me as the sunlight reflected off the white water. I knew it was my time. The gifts of the Holy Spirit confirmed it as well.

I had a prayer in my heart, and I felt my feet touch the cool, rolling water of the ocean. My mind had so many questions that I felt were still unanswered. My anxiety was rising, but I did my best to hold onto the words of the Lord. As I stepped into the water, I felt the pastor and two other good men walking beside me. I am not going to lie; I was a nervous wreck. I knew that getting baptized was the right thing for me, but doing this in front of what I felt was the entire continent of Africa was scary—like billions of people were witnesses to this simple, sacred act.

I am not comfortable being in front of people, but there I was in front of many who were all cheering me on. They were clearly excited, and I was about to faint. At the time, I still had no idea what the purpose of baptism was. I had many unanswered questions, but I knew God wanted this for me! I can't say that I noticed a change, and I think that is because when I was healed, I was anointed and the felt Holy Spirit at that time. It was like the baptism was merely another step of obedience.

However, as I walked out of the water, I was filled with an awareness of the following:

God had arranged for me to read a book about someone who experienced healing from Jesus.
God had blessed me with gifts of the Spirit to awaken me to help others and draw nearer to him.
God led me to pick that specific mission trip.
God told me the week before I left that I was going to be baptized!
God knew that one bridge would wash out so that we would be in the area.
God brought us closer to the ocean that day!
God planned for the sun to come out at just the right time!
God prompted a man to come up to me and say I would be baptized today!

When I think about all the things that God arranged just for me to be baptized, I am humbled. I now know why I needed to be baptized, and I understand why He arranged everything that happened. I don't know if I would have made the decision for baptism at that time, so He chose for me! All I know is that He called me to do His work, and that this was the next step for me in drawing closer to Him.

SECTION 3

FEARLESSLY STEPPING INTO THE CALLING

CHAPTER 9
BRAVE LIKE ESTHER— FOLLOWING THE CALL

Prayer:

Father,

I want to become who You created me to be, to resist the temptation to compare myself to others. Help me see the ways You have made me unique to serve You and Your Kingdom. Thank You for making me just as I am. Forgive me for the ways I have compared myself to the abilities of others. I pray that starting today, I would see the opportunities in front of me and use my gifts to be of service to others.

In Jesus' name,

Amen

* * *

Brave, bravery, courage, and courageous. When I think of these words, I think of another woman from the Bible—Esther. In the Old Testament, Esther lived in a time when Israel was in captivity. To summarize the story, she was merely an adopted daughter of a cousin, Mordecai, living in a foreign land. Mordecai worked for King Ahasuerus.

Esther had great beauty, but aside from that, she was an ordinary person in a sea of millions, like so many of us—everyday people doing everyday deeds, trying to make a difference in our own unique way. *God uses the ordinary person to make an extraordinary difference.*

In Esther 2, a decree was sent out to all the land:

8 "When the king's order and edict had been proclaimed, many young women were brought to the citadel of Susa and put under the care of Hegai. Esther also was taken to the king's palace and entrusted to Hegai, who had charge of the harem.

Esther had been warned by Mordecai not to reveal her heritage. (Esther 2:10).

Withholding her heritage was brave because there was a chance she would be killed if it was later discovered who she was. *Strength comes from God, not from man.* Mordecai promised to keep watch over her even though she was in the palace.

11 "Every day he walked back and forth near the courtyard of the harem, to find out how Esther was and what was happening to her."

Esther had someone who loved and cared for her and was there to be a guide as best he could for her. Soon it was time to enter into the presence of the King. Esther pleased him, and he made her his queen. (Esth. 2:17) Now, there is something important to note about becoming the queen regarding the law. If Esther had something to say to the king or would like to see him, she was not able to freely enter his presence without being summoned (Esther 4:11).

As the story continues, Haman, a leader in the king's court, became angry with Mordecai because he would not pay respect or bow to Haman. Therefore, Haman plotted to destroy Mordecai and *all the Jews* (Esther 3:4-6). Imagine being sought after and to have an entire nation be sentenced to die just because one person felt offended and slighted.

As knowledge of their grave danger unfolded for the Jewish people, Mordecai pled with Esther to seek help from the king. In Esther 4:14, it says:

> *"For if you remain silent at this time, relief and deliverance will arise for the Jews from another place, but you and your father's family will perish. And who knows but that you have come to your royal position for such a time as this?"*

Think about Esther's dilemma: It was against the law to approach the king without being summoned. Such an act was punishable by death. If she revealed who she was, a Jew, she may face execution. Either choice potentially doesn't have a great outcome. However, if she decided to remain quiet, she could, more than likely, enjoy a life of luxury and ease. She could live like the queen she was called to be. But there is something here that runs deep, and it is not that of ease and money. It is the family. If she chose the life of a queen, she would watch her family, the nation, and her people perish.

Esther's heart wasn't worried about herself; she felt the weight of the challenging problem the law presented. She asked Mordecai to gather all the Jews in Shushan and fast three days for her. She and her handmaids would do the same. In Esther 4:16, it says:

> *"When this is done, I will go to the king, even though it is against the law. And if I perish, I perish."*

She put all of her trust in God. Shouldn't we all do that? After three days of spiritually preparing herself, Esther approached the king. *With God, we step out in faith and fight our fears.* He received her. (Esther 5:2).

Esther invited the king and Haman to a feast she had arranged. She made sure that during the feast, she shared Haman's plot with the king, and Mordecai and her people were spared the death sentence. (Esther 6-7) Mordecai received high honors, and Haman got the punishment he had arranged for Mordecai. The courage and patience of Esther and Mordecai are an inspiration. *Patience is a blessing and a virtue that can be bestowed upon us.*

Esther's actions with God impacted and saved generations. *Esther, born for such a time, and with God, saved a nation.*

* * *

Since I was about 19, the enemy kept telling me that I was a *bad mom.* It was an awful, crushing, and never-ending feeling that weighed heavily on my heart—*mom guilt.* It kept me captive. I lived a life of shame and guilt for nearly four decades.

I did not want to reveal my true self because I was still listening to what the enemy was telling me. The devil knew that the way to keep me silent was through my children. He helped me believe the shame I felt for those many years: The shame of being teenage mom, having a child who couldn't be baptized, fighting with my husband, drinking, over-working, not being home when kids needed me, failing my first marriage and second marriages, more pain, and working to survive.

All of that was being heaped on me by the devil. He kept me from stepping out and telling my story. Even though I was healed in my physical body, the devil still knew my weakness. He knew that if I told my story of how Jesus showed up and defeated him, once again, that would take even more power from him. He was keeping me silent, and that kept people I could help from seeking their own deliverance.

Deliverance. This was what Esther did for her people, through the hand of God. I connect with the story of Esther because it took faith in God, fasting, and great courage to share with the man who could have killed her, the information that ended up saving a nation. God fearlessly chose Esther. Like Esther, I have been called—Fearlessly Chosen. Writing this entire story of being attacked by a demon is so that I could share with you my story of faith.

Part of this connection includes something from the past. Just like for Esther, not being able to share her heritage or her history, did not mean it would dictate her future. This is the same with me. How can these changes and recovery from the past happen? What is the cause of it? It is done through God—through Jesus Christ. Through Jesus, we can all be cleansed of our past. We will remember the pain of it less and less until it is gone.

Remembering a painful experience is terrible, and one that was with me for a long time is the fact that I drank. I know I shared a few little stories and hints through the book, but how did I change things? What happened? While the devil worked hard to keep me silent, Jesus worked harder to free me from the past—again, deliverance.

* * *

Sunny day, check. Sunscreen, check. Ice, food, coolers, check, check, check. Beer? Check! We were ready for another great family vacation, including a birthday afternoon and an evening at the beach with family and friends. The sunshine, the laughter of the grandkids, and the water created a great atmosphere. Still, I was never entirely comfortable with socializing unless I had a beer in my hand and a constant flow of alcohol pouring through me. So, I cracked another one open.

On the beach, we went skipping the waves in the ocean, laughing and playing. There was exuberant energy we could all feel. Crack, another beer. Somewhere around my fourth or fifth beer and the sun getting low, I was in that place where everything is funny and slow at the same time. It is a comfortable place for me. It means I will soon enter numbness, and all will be well.

We played more games, ate the rest of the food, and the sun began to dip toward the horizon. The afternoon was ending, the party on the beach would soon be over, and everyone would walk up to the house. My daughter and son in law packed things up and got ready to go. I found myself saying goodbye to them, but I was not prepared to go yet. When it was finally time to go up, the room was filled with people, celebrating around the dinner and cake my family had prepared for me. I guess during that time was when I said something in my drunken state to my cousin. We cut the birthday cake, I drank the last beer, and blacked out the party, falling into a 24-hour sleep. Who knows what I said to my cousin in that hazy near-comatose state? The words I shared did not stay in her confidence but found their way to my daughter. What did I say? It was something about my son-in-law, and it broke my daughter's heart. I don't even remember saying it and to this day do not know why I did.

A few days later, life was back to normal. Work, work, work, life, pain, more work, a few more days of the week passed, and soon we were nearing the weekend again. I called my daughter to catch up and see how she was. She was quiet, cold, and soon was off the phone. I did not know what had caused her shift in attitude. Maybe she was just having a bad day. A few days later she called me. "Mom, do you remember what happened at the beach last week?"

"Sure, we all had a great time at the beach," I answered.

"Do you remember anything at the end of the night?" my daughter asked with strength behind her words. I felt my face redden as my brain raced to the weekend and what I could have said. I had experienced this feeling numerous times before, so I knew it was not going to be good.

"Um, only that I said goodbye to y'all," I answered lamely, as I continued to push through the alcoholic memory loss. I could feel my color rise.

"There was more, Mom. You said words that cut deep." I could feel the tightness in my throat and the pain of my racing heart starting up again. I was overcome with profound regret.

"Mom, your words really hurt me. I have been fighting with myself all day to try to talk to you about this. I tried two or three times to just let it go, but dang, mom, you really messed up!" The tightness in my throat strangled me. I had no answer because I had no memory of the words. Each time I wracked my brain to see what I had said, I looked and looked, pushing through the cobwebs of my mind, only to arrive at an empty, blacked-out space with no answers.

Tears were beginning to well up, and I knew that I could not respond other than to say, "I'm sorry." My entire past life—of all the drinking and shame were being thrown back in my face. I was choking and drowning in a storm of emotion. I was not going to make it out on my own. I must face my past, but only God could clear the pain of it for me.

My daughter shared a few more choice words, but there was a shift inside me. I felt for the first time, the heat and light of the honesty of her words. It seemed they would burn holes in me and reveal my shame. Pain began to rise, and I felt the destroying force begin to battle within me. I looked at that dark place and felt the honesty of my daughter's words. I knew that I had to *quit* drinking. That was it. I. Must. Quit.

As my daughter saved me from destruction with alcohol, my son saved me from the destruction of guilt. Jacob has been through so much at a tender age. Mostly because I was still searching for my purpose, who I was, why I was here, and where I was going. He witnessed failed marriages, an overworked and underpaid mom—a drunk that burned the candle at both ends but could not find freedom from her pain. Watching that and experiencing it at such a young age, now at 18, Jacob had had enough. He moved in with my daughter and her husband. I was okay with that. He was taken care of there while I was able to pursue my goals, my interests, and another marriage. I traveled to Indiana to visit a new boyfriend. I left my dog with Jacob to watch. My dog was loyal to me, but not friendly to my son.

Following that visit to Indiana, I decided to move there with my boyfriend, without so much as having a conversation with Jacob. I just left. No conversation. Just emptiness. Why? I was so wrapped up in my brokenness that I didn't think about how anyone else was affected. All I had was pain—only for me and for no one else.

As a mother, once you become numb to the pain of others, it seems you have lost everything. I started to feel tension build up between Jacob and me. Phone calls were short, and texts were missed, and over time we were miles apart, physically and emotionally.

I wanted what I wanted, and I knew it was my fault. I loved my son, but I left him. He loved me but was disappointed in me. So who decides to show up? Satan. I listened to the enemy.

Worthless

Pathetic

Abandon your children for your desires

Distant

Cold

On and on piled the guilt of my mistakes. I knew if I didn't do something soon, it would destroy any hope of making amends with my son.

Where did I start? I started where I could, with pen and paper. I remember gathering sheets of paper underneath my hands and feeling the smooth, clean, lined surfaces, twirling a pen in my hand, and staring at the blank page. It was as if I could hear the kitchen clock ticking away the last bit of hope I had that this might work.

I finally grasped the pen and wrote, "Dear Jacob." It was as if the dam of emotions was released, and the waterworks began. My hand seemed to fly across the page, capturing and expressing my apology with cursive swirls and twists. I acknowledged and took responsibility for all of my wrongs. My hand began again on the top left of a page, and I worked left to right down, down, down the page, flip it over, and start again at the top corner. The paper began to be damp on the bottom right corner from my tears falling onto the page, warping it.

My apology turned into expressions of love for Jacob. I made lists and praised him for all the things he had done right, for the promises he kept, for all the things I had destroyed, yet he never gave up on me. Stroke after stroke, my hand continued across the pages until all I had inside of me was penned in the letter. I had released it all.

I folded the pages and tucked them into the envelope, sealed it, addressed it, and stamped it. That was it. It was finished. That letter changed our relationship forever. The hold that the devil had on me with my mom guilt was released. I was now free to step into my calling like Esther.

I gathered my courage; I dove into the work and started my deeper journey with God. It took a few months and years, but He changed it for me. Just like Esther, I knew that my *past would not dictate my future. It is still unwritten, and I can ask God to write a new future.* That was what he gave me.

* * *

Through my journey of faith, God showed me what I could do to help others. It is called CPIE: Called, Plan, Implement, Encourage.

C: Called. What passion has God laid on your heart that could change people's lives? What are you called to do?

After God healed me, He called me for something. I wanted to help people recover, body, soul, and spirit. I was passionate about opening a place to help not only survivors but also the people assisting others to improve. I needed to tell people how you can be sick from spiritual attack and how to prevent that from happening.

As I was studying the book of Esther, I was captivated by how God used her. The Holy Spirit showed me how to move forward and to help others learn from Esther's story.

He showed me that Esther first received her calling—saving the Jewish people. God placed her where she needed to be to do the will of her Father. I am sure it was not easy to overcome and do things I am sure she didn't feel prepared to do. But Esther did them because she was called and felt the passion for saving her people that He placed on her heart.

P: Plan. You have to make a plan once you figure out what God has called you to do.

Esther had a plan. She had everyone fast and pray. She planned how she was going to get a meeting with the King—how she would use the banquet to bring attention to Haman and his evil designs. It was during one of my prayer times that I felt God say I needed to sell my home and follow Him. I could not believe it because I had recently remodeled my home exactly how I wanted it. But before I knew what was happening, the house sold—part of the plan. Then I heard Him say to quit my job, so that is what I did, thinking that everything would work out immediately, but it was only a piece of the puzzle.

I: Implement. Once you have your plan, you have to have the courage to step out and do it just as Esther did. She sent word to Mordecai for all the Jews to fast for three days to strengthen her so that when she approached the king, she would be accepted. Implementing your plan takes action and courage. This was the hardest part for me because I was not sure what I needed to be doing. But every day, I did something to move me closer to what God had called me to do.

E: Encourage. To me, this is the most important part; God wants all his children to know Him and have a relationship with Him. He says, "Come, Follow me." Be encouraged to follow Him. He knows the way, and He wants you to follow. He wants to use you to help others. If you don't do what God has called you to do, how can you encourage others to do the same?

Be brave and dare to step out as Esther did. We each must face our calling from God.

CHAPTER 10
STAY ON THE PATH

Prayer:

God, Help us. Where we are weak; make us strong.
Where we are wavering help us lay our anchor down.
May we find our strength in You. You are so believable;
we see Your hand in everything. May we never feel the
pangs of condemnation. We want nothing that is not
associated with You; it will only leave us empty. Give us
strength and increase our faith. Make us into warriors
that don't back down. You are the answer to everything.
In Jesus' name, I pray.
Amen

* * *

First, God divided the light from the darkness, making day and night. The second day He organized the Heavens and the earth. On the third day, He divided the land from the waters and created grass, flowers, trees, fruit, and herbs. Next, the Father created the sun, moon, and stars on the fourth day. The fish and fowl were created on the fifth day. Then a stunning achievement happened on the sixth day—Jesus Christ created the animals. Following the end of that day, Heavenly Father created man "in his own image, he created them; male and **female he** created them." (Genesis 1:27; emphasis added).

Genesis 2:22 says:

"Then the Lord God made a woman from the rib he had taken out of the man, and he brought her to the man."

Taking the rib is significant because man and woman are meant to be side by side. It is a partnership. It is a relationship. We are to live, work, and play side by side. Eve came to life as a helper and as a partner. She was to help build and organize the creation of the bodies of man. She was designed by God to conceive and nurture life. Eve is the first of all women. She labored beside her companion:

"Nevertheless, in the Lord woman is not independent of man, nor is man independent of woman." (1 Corinthians 11:11)

Eve is the great link in the chain of creation. In Genesis 2 it says:

18 "The Lord God said, 'It is not good for the man to be alone. I will make a helper suitable for him.'

19 "Now the Lord God had formed out of the ground all the wild animals and all the birds in the sky. He brought them to the man to see what he would name them; and whatever the man called each living creature, that was its name.

20 "So the man gave names to all the livestock, the birds in the sky and all the wild animals. But for Adam no suitable helper was found.

21 "So the Lord God caused the man to fall into a deep sleep; and while he was sleeping, he took one of the man's ribs and then closed up the place with flesh.

22 "Then the Lord God made a woman from the rib he had taken out of the man, and he brought her to the man.

23 "The man said,
'This is now bone of my bones
and flesh of my flesh;
she shall be called "woman,"
for she was taken out of man.'"

Female. We know her as Eve. She was given a title and is known as the *"mother of all living."* (Genesis 3:20). That title is a powerful one. According to the definition from the Merriam Webster Dictionary of "mother," it means the following: a woman in authority, a female parent, maternal tenderness or affection, to give birth to, to give rise to, to bear. But in scripture, it is fully understood to be the *mother of all living.* That means to give life, to co-create with Deity.

When I think of Eve, I have deep feelings of love, sympathy, and empathy. She had a critical job to do to be the mother of all living, but there was a process that had to happen for this title to be fulfilled. In Genesis 3, we read:

1 "Now the serpent was more crafty than any of the wild animals the Lord God had made. He said to the woman, 'Did God really say, "You must not eat from any tree in the garden?"'

2 "The woman said to the serpent, 'We may eat fruit from the trees in the garden,

3 'but God did say, "You must not eat fruit from the tree that is in the middle of the garden, and you must not touch it, or you will die."

4 'You will not certainly die,' the serpent said to the woman.

5 'For God knows that when you eat from it your eyes will be opened, and you will be like God, knowing good and evil.'"

According to Genesis 3:6, when the woman saw that the fruit of the tree was good for food and pleasing to the eye, and also desirable for gaining wisdom, she took some and ate it. I wanted to see if there was more.

13 "Then the Lord God said to the woman, 'What is this you have done?' The woman said, 'The serpent deceived me, and I ate.'"

Reading it in The King James Version of the Bible, it says:

13 "And the Lord God said unto the woman, 'What is this that thou hast done?' And the woman said, 'The serpent beguiled me, and I did eat.'"

Deceived and beguiled. Those are fascinating words.

In the Cambridge English dictionary, to *deceive* means to persuade someone that something false is the truth, or to keep the truth hidden from someone for your advantage. This is a powerful word that shows how Eve was given information that created conflict with the commandment she was given from God, and what the serpent/Satan was saying to her. To persuade someone, it may take many hours, meetings, days, or weeks of providing evidence for someone else to start to believe the lie.

Eve must have been in conflict over this. She wanted to follow God's commandment, and yet she had been deceived and beguiled. She wrestled with what to do, how to do it, and what would be the consequence for eating the fruit. I can feel this pain with her. I can't imagine having to choose to follow God, knowing that you need to multiply and replenish the earth, but also knowing that if you eat from the tree, you will die. But now someone tells you won't die; you will be like the Gods, knowing good from evil. This is a deep conflict.

Thinking about this conflict in one more step is to think about Jesus. Jesus is the central figure in the whole plan of salvation. He was set before the world in Heavenly Father's plan as the one to save the world. Think about this: Eve had to make a choice (and she struggled with it) to eat of the fruit so that the posterity of mankind could be born. But with that choice, they would be cast out of the Garden of Eden, and she, Adam, and their future children would then need to rely on a Savior, the Son of Man, the Lord of Hosts, the Holy One of Israel, to make it back to Heavenly Father.

Jesus was prepared to take on this role. But still, to be Eve and know that your choice was what would start it all in motion, must have been a heavy burden. Jesus was willing, ready, and able to take on this role of Savior. It was His mission, and He has fulfilled it; we just need to accept it.

As a result of eating from the tree of knowledge, Eve and Adam were cast from the beautiful garden, a place of safety and of being with God, into a world of struggle. For Eve, they had to leave the Garden and experience a new concept of pain, toil, trials, and labor. One of Eve's experiences was to bear children. (Genesis 3:16-17). But we know that Jesus Christ was the key to helping them while they were here on earth. Jesus is the way.

Since the fall, all humanity has been born to billions of women who have experienced conception, labor, and delivery. They know the *pain* of bearing children. Childbirth helped save my life, because it was through my sin that God saved me. I was pregnant at age 18, and I know that my daughter was a gift from God.

To me, labor pains are a gift—an offering to help us appreciate the life with which He blesses us. But I also understand that my daughter saved me another way, through a different kind of labor pain. According to Genesis 3:6, when the woman saw that the fruit of the tree was good for food and pleasing to the eye, and also desirable for gaining wisdom, she took some and ate it.

I have been tempted many times by what is pleasing to the eye, but what I find fascinating is that Satan has been here since the beginning of time, with the first man and woman. His one goal is to defeat God's plan by tempting us with that forbidden fruit. I love that God spoke about Eve's vulnerability. It shows that no one is perfect when Satan decides to focus on us. I was that person, like Eve, who Satan tempted with forbidden fruit. I chose to eat it instead of looking to God and what He wanted me to do.

I chose to pick the forbidden fruit at a young age. I was seventeen when I decided to have sex outside of marriage. I decided to follow my ways instead of God's ways. I was pregnant at the age of 18 and unwed. My boyfriend was at home while I was in college. I partied one night to the point that I passed out on a curb on the side of the street. I have no idea how I got there, but the next thing I remember was walking into my dorm room and my friend hollering at me.

A few weeks later, I walked into the campus clinic and came out knowing I was nine-weeks pregnant. The drinking, the partying, and college was now suspended. In a rush and with no real excitement, her father and I were married, and college was a distant memory.

Eve was strengthened through her pain, not despite it. We all sin, but it's about what we do with the wrongdoing that matters. I chose to look to Eve as a heroine; because of her, we have the gift of labor pain. Pain that only women can experience. Only women can produce fruit because of it.

God also gave Eve the power to crush the head of the enemy, and all we receive is a bruised heel. That's it. (Genesis 3:15)

I see Eve as a woman that Satan chose, thinking she was weak. But instead, God used that weakness and made her strong. She passed this down through generations to come. Satan tried to defeat me because of my faults, but God made me strong through the labor pains of not only bearing my children but also the journey of life.

Eve, as the first woman, forged the way for all of us to be saved through the process of creation with deity, that we get to see very clearly the opportunity not only to be a co-creator but a deliverer of life. I thank Eve for not running away from her calling. Her mission was to start the entire human family, and she did not stray from that path. She was *fearlessly chosen*, and she accepted.

Many women in the scriptures, women I know personally, and women who are a part of my life have experienced pain, shame, labor, struggle, tough decisions, and even abuse. Yet, I see these same women finding love, light, and hope in Jesus. I find them looking beyond these circumstances and pushing through their challenges so they can find that hope. As I studied more women in the scriptures, another woman came to mind.

* * *

Hagar was an obedient woman, yet she had some fear. She was willing but needed to know that God was there for her. We know that God had promised Abram he would have a son. Genesis 16 holds a lot of pieces of the story, but what I want to focus on is the pains of my heart for Hagar.

She was a slave, then taken as a wife to follow the laws and customs so that an heir could be born to her master. Hagar was obedient and followed instruction. She conceived and had a baby. This was when things turned. Sarai felt jealous and made a choice. In Genesis 16, she took matters into her own hands. Sarai mistreated Hagar:

> 6 *"'Your slave is in your hands,' Abram said. 'Do with her whatever you think best.' Then Sarai mistreated Hagar; so she fled from her."*

Hagar fled to a spring on the way to Shur. The road through Shur was in the direction toward Egypt. She was on her way home—to freedom! God sent an angel to find Hagar. (See, I know God knows us and what we need). The angel of the Lord found her by the spring.

The Lord knows all of our actions, whether we believe in Him or not. Jesus knows we are going to make mistakes, will be hurt, and will need to learn lessons of love and forgiveness to follow Him. So just like Hagar, He sent an angel to her:

> 8 *"And he said, "Hagar, slave of Sarai, where have you come from, and where are you going? I'm running away from my mistress, Sarai, she answered."*

Sarai had poorly treated Hagar. That was why she ran away. God saw that mistreatment. I know God was ready to help Hagar, even though she did not believe in Him the same way Sarai did. He is there for all of His children, even when the worst things like slavery and abuse happen.

Like Hagar, I know the feeling of abuse, the sting of rebuke, and being hated for doing what you were told to do—especially when you had no choice. Watching others suffer through the pain of slavery and being forced to do things that are against their will pulls at my heart. It is dehumanizing.

Hagar, as a slave, was humiliated, and God knew that, yet he sent the angel to instruct her to return to Sarai—the very person who mistreated her. However, there is something big here. God gives her a promise:

10 "I will increase your descendants so much that they will be too numerous to count."

This was a promise to console, comfort, and encourage her, and hopefully help her to return to Sarai. In verse 11, the Lord heard Hagar's misery. Heavenly Father knew Hagar, just as He knows each one of us. He knows the pain of slavery, the heartache of returning to it, and the sacrifice it was for Hagar to go back to a place of potential abuse and mistreatment. But there is a vast promise here:

12 "He will be a wild donkey of a man; his hand will be against everyone and everyone's hand against him, and he will live in hostility toward all his brothers."

A wild donkey? When we think about donkeys, we think about stubborn animals, that are maybe even a little ugly. That doesn't sound like a great promise. But if donkeys are wild, they are free. They are not in captivity.

Hagar was a slave and would be her whole life, but because of her sacrifice and her willingness to bear hardship, her son would be free. What a great blessing was given to Hagar, that her son would not know slavery and that his people would be free! This was meant to be a message of hope, joy, and liberation.

Finally, in verse 13, Hagar says:

"'You are the God who sees me,' for she said, 'I have now seen the One who sees me.'"

She knew that God saw her. How many of you have had that feeling of God *seeing* you? Have you felt examined (flaws, mistakes, and all), and yet you still feel His love after that?

I have felt that love, as I shared in Chapter 7, when I was healed and encompassed with light. I think about the warmth

I felt, and I know Hagar must have felt God's arms around her, hearing and caring for her. She had personal interaction with God and knew her son would be set free. Her story is one of love, devotion, and great sacrifice.

Hagar was chosen and stayed on the path. Eve was called by God as well. How many of you have felt the way Eve and Hagar did? You have been chosen to do something and yet you are second-guessing yourself. You are scared to follow through. You are wondering why God chose you.

I wondered why I was chosen as Eve was, being so close to God, who knew she would make the choice to allow all of humankind to fall. I was given the chance to know God as she and Hagar did. I can identify well with both of them in the sense that when we are called to do something challenging and difficult but follow through and do it anyway, it is the power of being *fully chosen*.

Jesus knows and loves you, as He knows Eve and Hagar. He knows me and you. He is the one who calls us to do great things. Many times, we may be afraid. In that fear, we may make mistakes instead of seeking Him. But like Eve, through childbearing, she found light and connection with God. And like Hagar, sometimes he sends angels into your path. Our angels can be the *everyday people* who cross our way. But like Eve and Hagar, if we stay on the path, we will find our way— our way back to God.

End notes: https://dictionary.cambridge.org/us/dictionary/english/deceive

https://www.interserveusa.org/gods-promise-to-hagar-clearing-up-a-misunderstaning/

CHAPTER 11
ME FIRST

Prayer:

Lord,
I want to move forward and take hold of all that you offer
me. Help me release all that hinders my spiritual growth
and help me develop an intimate relationship with You. I
open my heart, my eyes and my hands to everything You
have for me to find complete healing in You.
In Jesus' name,
Amen

* * *

What an intriguing title: *ME FIRST*. Think about this phrase when you read Matthew 6:33:

> *"But seek first his kingdom and his righteousness,*
> *and all these things will be given to you as well."*

Think about what he is asking. He is asking you to seek Him first in all things. Why? What is the blessing? He is promising you that if you put God first, the rest will be blessed.

God will add more and more to you as you place Him first. What a gift! What a blessing! This has been a huge theme for this entire book. Look at all the stories I have shared with you. As I finally learned about how to place Him first, I then became first.

Now, look at this pattern. As we seek Him, we are filled with love and knowledge. In that love, we become a priority as well. It is not selfish to put yourself as a priority; this is the act of self-care.

What is self-care? Is it the act of taking care of yourself before caring for others? I have shared my story to show you my journey toward healing. We all need healing, and the degree that I needed it was intense. I had demons enter into my body because they have no body, and they want that. However, I was also making terrible choices. I was lost to the power of God, and mostly feared God or did not believe that healing or salvation was for me, a sinner. Satan had a hold of my soul; my body was physically ill from it, and my spirit was numb to the direction I should go.

However, Jesus never gave up on me but pressed the learning and healing on my heart. 1 Thessalonians 5:

> 23 *"May God Himself, the God of peace, sanctify you through and through. May your whole spirit, soul and body be kept blameless at the coming of our Lord Jesus Christ.*
>
> 24 *"The one who calls you is faithful, and He will do it."*

This is the scripture that led me to complete healing—to understanding what that means, and how important it is to pay attention to all of your body, not just your physical self.

115

On my journey to find answers for my healing, but also to help me understand the gifts that I was blessed with, I attended a Divine Healing Conference. I had never witnessed healing lines or anything remotely like it, so I was intrigued from the start.

As I sat listening, taking notes on all the scriptures about healing and trying to understand how Jesus is still healing today, I knew I was healed but I still looked for confirmation of what had happened. I sat at a table with two different ladies. One was quiet, and I could see deep pain in her eyes. I didn't know her or her story.

The other lady was her friend, and she was suffering from physical back pain, but she was upbeat and full of life; I didn't see pain in her eyes. At this time, I did not suffer from any kind of pain, so when the call came to step forward to the healing line, I just sat there and watched. Both ladies at my table stepped forward to go receive their healing. I knew instantly which of my new friends would be healed and which wouldn't.

How did I know this? I knew because of my experience that physical healing is possible, but the journey in spiritual healing is found in the process and also from the Holy Spirit. I knew the lady with just the back pain would be healed, but the other lady with so much soul pain would not.

The next morning my friend with the back pain was healed—no more pain. Her friend was not healed, but she said she was not giving up and was still praying for healing. I quietly added her to my prayers, as well.

The next healing session started with a question raised by one of the participants, "Why do so many of the same people keep going through the healing lines?" The speaker from the stage could not answer, but I knew. why my friend beside me would not find healing even though she was going from line to line. Her physical pain was caused by a spiritual and soulful problem, not merely a physical problem. She needed to be healed from the inside out just as I was. We can try healing our physical bodies all day long, but if we do not deal with the emotional, spiritual pain, we will never find complete healing.

I have shared the story of my seven-year journey to find healing— how the demons were cast out. I was released from that darkness by Jesus Himself as He stretched His hands toward me. The very hands that bore the mark of the crucifixion poured light into each cell of my entire body, and I was cleansed and purified. I was freed physically—from pain, the aches, my racing heart, jerking limbs, pain in my head, my restricted voice, breathing challenges, and smelly sweats.

This was only part of my journey. Weeks and weeks following the miracle, I still remembered feeling strangely empty, like something was missing. Through the help of incredible, faith-filled leaders, I began to read the Bible and put forth diligent effort in finding God. I know that sounds like a contradiction, but I learned that I had only been partially healed. I still needed to seek His grace and daily forgiveness for my mistakes.

You see, the underlying cause of my disease was that I did not have my mind and soul focused on God. I was good at one thing. I had shame because I didn't understand compassion for the sinner—me. With that judgment I found blame right along with it, which is lacking compassion for the other guy. I blamed everything or everyone else for my circumstances. And I was a victim of everything.

In my journal, I wrote:

"The shame that I was held in was the foothold Satan needed to control my life. God wants more from me, but first, my soul needed to be liberated from the shame, the guilt that had controlled my life for days, weeks, months, and years. I was physically sick, but even after healing, I was not fully whole until I relied on God for the full healing. We must be healed, body, soul, and spirit."

How do we find that full healing? To be a servant of Christ, you have to be able to prepare yourself to hold His light. This is done through a method of self-care God gave me during prayer, pondering, and seeking Him.

Self-care has many shapes, forms, rhythms, and routines. You know the timing of your day, the needs of your family, and the desires of your heart. I want you to know that you have the freedom to find what works for you. But here are the essential parts to remember: **ME FIRST**.

Wait. What? That seems to be very selfish, not self-care. Let me share with you how God showed it to me. **ME FIRST** is the following:

M - Meditate on God.
E - Exercise and Eat well.

F - Forgiveness/Fear/but with Faith we change.
I - I am who God says I am.
R - Rest.
S - Sustainability. God wants us to prosper, which means you have to receive to give.
T - Transform.

M - Meditate on God. Meditation can take any form that you know will work for you, but the importance is that you think, ponder, and pray about the things of God first in your life. If He is the center of your life, balance is achieved. You will be able to handle and find His peace when Satan throws his fiery darts at you. Trials, mistakes, anger, guilt, and shame are a part of life and will continue to happen, but you get better at not dwelling in shame and guilt when you are with God. The depths of the trials can be *mitigated* as you *meditate* on God first. If you put God first, He will put you first.

E - Exercise. I am not a fitness coach or expert, but what I know is that our bodies were built to move. They were created to enjoy the movement of limbs, the feeling of running, walking, hiking, stretching, swimming, gardening, working, and many other physical activities. When we are in movement and motion, our minds are free to think clearly; our brain receives more oxygen, filling it with better thoughts. The benefit is that as we engage both body and mind, it begins to heal our soul.

Eating is the concept of eating clean whole foods—foods that come from God and are not manufactured by man. Listen to your body and find a pathway that helps your body feel clean with energy. I know the foods that help me feel this way, and I know the foods that don't. The search is to find your pathway, the nutrition that is right for your body. This is excellent self-care; many foods can be added to the diet for healing and better energy.

F - Forgiveness, Fear, but with Faith we are changed. Forgiveness is daily asking to be pardoned from the poor choices we make, be they big or small. Jesus' power of forgiveness is absolute and can save us all. Our efforts to be close to Jesus rely on a desire to be forgiven of our shortcomings. God, in turn, asks us to be kind and compassionate with ourselves. We also share a willingness to forgive others, to give them the benefit of the doubt, to not judge, as in condemnation, but to offer His grace through our forgiveness of them.

Do you seek daily forgiveness from God and from yourself? Do you daily forgive others?

The second part of this step is to be filled with *Faith* and not fear. Faith and fear are on opposite sides of a spectrum. You cannot be fearful and be faithful at the same time. One is of God, and one is of the devil. So when you feel fear, think about why you are having that fear: why you are worried, why you are hesitating to do something for someone else, or why you are not following your dreams and purpose. If it is because of fear, remember:

"There is no fear in love. But perfect love drives out fear..."
(1 John 4:18)

Do you walk in faith or fear?

I - I am who Gods says I am. It is a journey and a process. How many of you like to hike—the dirt, the rocks, and the good earth beneath your feet? The smell of pine, the crisp air filling your lungs, and the forward motion of your body are refreshing. As you step, push, and strain up steep hills to find the view, you notice that you climbed at your pace. You may have started your hike hours ago and only gotten 1 mile. Others may have passed you along the path, or the opposite might have happened. Either way, our journey on the hike is what teaches us the lessons.

It is not a race or competition. If we are at the trailhead just starting, if we have been hiking for days, or if we are nearing the summit, it is similar to our relationship with God. We start where we are found. Not where anyone else is, but only where we are. God knows our hearts, and if we trust in Him, our *walk* with Him will be at the right place, at the right time, and for the right reason.

Where are you in your relationship with God?

R - Rest. God showed me the importance of rest after I quit my job. I thought, *Okay, God, I have done what you asked me to do so let's do this great thing you promised me.* I thought I was ready to move into the next phase of my journey with God. But little did I know that was not His plan.

After a month of not working and starting to freak out about living in a camper, I was ready to give up and go back to work. Was I giving up on God or was I giving up on myself?

I think I was giving up on both. I was not prepared for this new challenge. The days of seeing the same four walls of the camper and the lack of things on my schedule were driving me to revisit my decision to quit working. It's like I quit before I considered how my life would look. Now that I had a taste of it, I felt a fear of being lazy, of not producing, or being idle. I had always worked, doing what it took to get things done, sometimes working two to three jobs to pay the bills. Not working seemed ridiculous to me, and a foggy, hazy doubt started to darken my thoughts.

Each day the walls of the small camper were closing in. I prayed and prayed. I needed hope that what I had done in following His will was right. Another week had rolled by when I felt God tell me, "Be still and know that I am God." (Psalm 46:10). His words then were, *"You never stopped and spent time with Me!"*

You never stopped and spent time with Me! This echoed in my heart and head while kneeling in my small new life. I stopped. Sound seemed to stop. Time stopped. I was to rest from my work and cares, to be with God. To spend real time with Him, His word, power in Him—all meaning finding rest in Him. The answer filled me with sweet love and gentle light, and I knelt in the camper by my bed. I had an answer.

I got off my knees and began to open my journals and the scriptures. I found times where I pled for answers and rest. That admonition led me to look into the word, and I discovered that even Jesus took time to rest. I lifted my eyes from the print and allowed His gentleness to encompass me, calm me, and still me. From that moment on, I spent time with God, in His counsel, listening to Him—retraining my brain to know that it is okay to rest—to give up control and let God take care of me.

This brought me to meditation. I understood how import-ant it was because when I was healed I was told to read the Bible. I'd felt it was a waste of my time, so when I found myself at my lowest and knew I could not go another day of pain and sorrow, I decided to go to the Bible again. This time I started praying before I read. Praying aligned my will to God's. Staying attuned to His will meant that I needed to listen to the directions He was giving me. Listening was an important part. Instead of doing all the talking, I became quiet. I focused on what I thought the Holy Spirit was saying to me through the scriptures. It was life-changing, and I have lived my life since by not only praying but listening and receiving through meditating on the Word of God.

S - Sustainability. When I quit my job, I thought God wanted me to be poor to follow Him. I always thought that having money damned people from going to heaven. I thought that you were only allowed in if you gave up everything. It was the only way to follow Him. When I quit my job, it was with the intent that I was going to follow Him, and that poverty was the only true route. I thought that was why God told me to quit my job to follow Him.

Look at this scripture in Matthew 19:24:

> *"Again I tell you; it is easier for a camel to go through the eye of a needle than for someone who is rich to enter the kingdom of God."*

I thought prosperity, wealth, and luxury were sins. If our *focus* is only in gaining and wanting, we will forget to serve and love others. In Matthew 6:21, it says:

> *"For where your treasure is, there your heart will be also."*

Was I fixed on being wealthy, or providing for my family's needs? It wasn't about being rich or poor, but where my heart was. Even if you are poor in heart, you may always be wanting and coveting. That's not good either. I continued to search and find meaning for prosperity, and I was led to 2 Corinthians 9:11:

> *"You will be enriched in every way so that you can be generous on every occasion, and through us your generosity will result in thanksgiving to God."*

After reading this multiple times, I became aware that prosperity is not about attaining wealth or living a life of luxury but about thriving as the person God created you to be.

Sustainability is the ability to live within our means. To me, sustainability is the prosperity that God provides for you to do what He has called you to do. If it means giving you a lot so you can give back a lot for His glory, then that is what He will provide. If it means giving you a small amount to give back a tiny amount, that is what He will provide. Our wealth comes from Him and He wants to give it to us, so He may establish His covenant through us.

He wants us to be able to sustain a way of life to give Him glory. He did not ask me to quit my job to be impoverished. He asked me to quit so He could provide everything I needed to glorify Him in every way. He sustains me by giving me everything I need to give to others.

T - Transformation. In anything we do with God, a portion of it will be the transformation we want to be a part of. It was through ME FIRST that I was transformed to be the person that God wanted. It was a process and a journey to let go and let God. He says, "*I Am*," not, "who I *say* I am." I am now made new to do what He has called me to do. Be prepared to be changed in your heart, your body, your soul, and your spirit. Be ready for a transformational journey and growing pains. When you are feeling it, you'll know you are on the right path. Don't quit because it is hard. Don't ever leave!

This is how we build a strong foundation; the enemy cannot defeat us if we center our faith in Jesus Christ. God gives us second chances; He gave me one for sure. It is up to me to become stronger, healthier, and to use this second chance to be who He called me to be. I can't do that without putting myself first—to walk in the way of the Lord.

Even on your journey with God, you will mess up. You will stumble, but God will extend His right hand and pull you up. I wish I could say that after I was healed it was easy, but it wasn't. Thankfully, God sustained me as I kept moving forward every step of the way. Genesis 50:

20 "You intended to harm me, but God intended it for good to accomplish what is now being done, the saving of many lives.

21 "So then, don't be afraid."

This is what God did for me. He took something the devil meant for harm and used it for good to accomplish what is now being done. It took me walking through all the steps of ME FIRST to be transformed to do what He has called me to do, by finding complete healing in body, soul, and spirit.

God will take that and use it for good if you can just hang in there, keep moving forward, get up every day, and reach to God. At first, I kept all my pain to myself; I didn't know what to do or how to move forward. I didn't have a book or documentary to help me. I had to depend on God to help me discover my way in Jesus. I simply never gave up and kept looking forward, no matter how hard it was.

Jesus never gave up on me, even when I denied Him. He helped me build a strong foundation in Him and prepared me to fight all the battles ahead. Why? Because I have been Fearlessly Chosen. If you and I step out in faith and give hope to others out of love, then we are doing what Jesus has called us to do.

CHAPTER 12

FEARLESSLY CHOSEN: WHY ME? WHY NOT ME! WHY NOT YOU?

Prayer:

Heavenly Father,
We thank You that You hold the victory over sin and death in this world. We thank You that You came to set the captives free. We thank You for the freedom and the hope You bring. Thank You for Your greatness when I was weak and for choosing me when I was discouraged. I pray that with Your strength and guidance, I will walk this path of righteousness until You take me home.
In Jesus' name,
Amen

* * *

There were three main questions through my entire healing journey: 1) Why *me*? 2) Why *not* me! And 3) Why not *you*? Following those questions, three clarifying thoughts came to me. The concept and idea of being delivered, liberated, forgiven, and of the importance of the Holy Spirit.

WHY ME?

It is a cry that is in my heart far too often. Generally, it comes from not feeling worthy or not being strong enough to complete a task that is in front of me. That feeling of not being able to do things made me feel trapped. I felt stuck, and when I felt that way, I made terrible choices. The cry, *why me,* also felt like God was pulling me out of a crowd and having me stand up for all to see. I didn't like to have a lot of attention drawn to me because I felt flawed and that all were mocking me—why me?

I am much more comfortable with putting my head down and going to work. I'm more of a *get-things-done-behind-the-scenes* type of gal. However, when God wants you to do things, there is nothing that will stop Him. I had to address the challenge of my desire to be behind the scenes, trapped, and stuck. How did I learn to share my testimony? It is simple. Trust Him. This is the only thing that leads to true liberation. What does it mean to liberate your soul? It means freedom from sin, making poor choices, pain, and shame.

I was praying one day about something, and I felt God leading me to the account of Mary Magdalene. I shared her story briefly in a previous chapter but feel compelled to emphasize that she had a tremendous role in my healing and understanding of what happened to me. When I read that she, too, had been delivered from demons, and that Jesus healed her, it gave me validation regarding what happened to me. I could relate to her; I understood her pain.

The next part of her story said that when she was delivered, her soul was liberated. I thought, *wow, that is precisely what happened to me.* Like Mary, who was liberated from all the demons and set free to follow Jesus, to be one of His strongest supporters, I too, know the meaning of liberation. She never left Jesus or faltered. He even came to her, making her the first to witness the Resurrected Lord.

Why me? It is simple; I am worth it. I know I am. How do I know? Because I felt of His love for me during my healing, the same love that He wants you to feel. It was glorious to know that I am worthy of His love and that when you come to Him, you can feel the depth of this blessing, too. What power! I know He has a plan for me and you when we trust in Him as Mary did, as we are blessed with His love.

* * *

WHY NOT ME?

In Acts 13:38, it reads:

> *"Therefore, my friends, I want you to know that through Jesus the forgiveness of sins is proclaimed to you."*

Forgiveness is an incredible gift, although I struggled with the concept for decades. I hadn't quite understood how much God wants us to forgive others and ourselves until one day He showed me.

He had recently revealed something traumatic to me. It was something that happened in my childhood that I had blocked for 52 years. He showed it to me because it was keeping me from finding complete healing. I asked God, "Why now? Why, after all these years, do you choose now to show me this? How do you expect me to move on?" I could feel God. I felt Him right next to my face. It seemed I could feel His breath on my face, and He answered me. I heard, *"He repented. I forgave him, and you will too!"*

My very breath caught in my throat, and time was suspended. All I could feel was the steady beating of my calm heart. Then I felt warmth begin to fill my soul like a soft wind brushing across my senses. I was consumed with an understanding of what forgiveness means. It's a feeling for all who have repented; we ask for that beautiful sweetness to be part of our lives. I finally understood completely! I thought, *Wow, God is serious about forgiveness!*

It is one of the most critical parts of being able to walk with God. We must forgive everyone, no matter what has been done to us. I was thinking back to how many times I had asked God to forgive me for all that I had done, and I knew in my heart that I was unconditionally forgiven. I had to forgive this person at this time.

I knew it was time to forgive and let go. No more going back and revisiting the pain of the past, because it has been swept away in Christ Jesus! It was true forgiveness. I began to feel the same, sweeping away all the wrongs I had committed in my life! I am free from pain I held onto that I didn't even know about. Matthew 6:

14 "For if you forgive other people when they sin against you, your Heavenly Father will also forgive you,

15 "But if you do not forgive others their sins, your Father will not forgive your sins."

As we seek God and repent of our sins, we are forgiven. As a result of gratitude for freedom from guilt and shame, many people feel called to serve God. In John 15:16, it says:

"You did not choose me, but I chose you and appointed you so that you might go and bear fruit—fruit that will last—and so that whatever you ask in my name the Father will give you."

This scripture helped me understand my journey of healing. It was the answer to my prayers and so many other things I hadn't understood before. I was chosen, so the question of *Why not me?* was finally answered. I am worthy of being accepted. I am worthy of His love. I am worthy of being healed and now helping others as well. I knew then that Jesus chose me for this exact purpose. This is the only explanation I have. I was not actively seeking Jesus at the time, but He was already seeking me.

* * *

Why Not You? Jesus has saved us and called us to a holy life—not because of anything we have done but because of His own purpose and grace. One of the callings I felt the Lord pulling me toward was to go to Africa. By this time, I knew the feeling of the Holy Spirit, and what would happen when I chose to follow Him instead of arguing with Him. When I did this, my life was always better. The most incredible part about going on this trip was that I didn't question why I was going across the world to do something I had never dreamed of doing before. I simply stepped forward with faith.

Upon arriving at the airport in Africa, I immediately noticed the difference in culture. They were nothing like the American airports. No luxury, fancy bathrooms, or comfortable seats like the typical American airport has. Yet I was still excited and knew I was there for a reason.

We traveled on a bus for several hours until we reached our first stop to eat. All the way there I was taking in the unique scenery and marveling at the difference in landscape, but nothing could have prepared me for what I saw in this town. We pulled in and everywhere around us was dirt, buildings with no windows, dozens of people standing around talking, and armed guards walking around.

I stared out the window in shock at what I saw, and I said, "God, you chose the wrong woman for this." As I said this to myself, I was trying to figure out how to get the bus to take me back to the airport. I was on the verge of a breakdown; I honestly thought this was something I could not do. Why in the world would God choose something like this for me? I had already been healed and experienced so much, but this was more than what I thought I could do.

But off the bus I went because I had no way of getting back to the airport. We had to put our backpacks in front of us so no one would steal things, and on top of that, as I was walking into the "restaurant," I passed a person with several little pigs that looked like they had been deep-fried, lying there on the counter. I thought, *there is no way I can do this.* Entering the restaurant, all I could see was dirt and animals roaming around. I guess by this time I was in shock.

I asked where the bathroom was and discovered it was a room with merely a hole in the ground. One of the locals walked in on me while I was squatting. I was about in tears by this time. Why me? Yes, this question was rising up in my thoughts! I wanted just to get out and get away. When I walked out, I was not expecting to have a little boy of about ten years old walk up to me.

He had the most beautiful smile I had ever seen, and he started talking to me in English. His smile and his gentleness brought peace and comfort to me. I knew in that moment God was showing why He chose me. He showed me that all people need love and have love to give. Just as the Father says, *"He will never leave me nor forsake me."* After my encounter with that lovely boy, my desire to run away vanished. I saw beauty everywhere, the buildings, the landscape, but most importantly, the people. I fell in love with everything about Africa and cannot wait to go back.

* * *

God showed me how much strength I had on that trip. He also showed me that the voice I heard before the trip was the

Holy Spirit. I felt compelled to begin a search and study of my life from when I first felt the feeling of the Holy Spirit. I went back to my journals and read and reread all the times that influence was there. As my eyes pored over the pages, it became clear to my heart how the Spirit spoke to me. I now recognize that voice, and I trust it to lead me where He needs me to be.

The Holy Spirit was *The Voice* I heard during Reiki before I went to Africa. It was the voice that told me to sell my house and quit my job. The Holy Spirit has been my helper all along, and He wanted to show me how important He is. When I heard the Holy Spirit say to me as I lay on the treatment table that *Great things would come from this,* and *This isn't just about you anymore,* I knew I could not quit and run back to my comfort zone, but that I must keep going. That thought liberated me.

I know that with the power of the Spirit, our healing from sin and physical pain never stops. We have to go out and tell our stories of how Jesus saved and healed us so that our healing can continue. When God chooses you, it will not be easy. You will want to give up sometimes, but He always shows His loving care in some way. It usually comes as tender mercies during the everyday activities of our lives, for that is where we live.

* * *

One time I was sitting in Goodyear to get my tires changed, and I was reading something on my phone, when a lady that was sitting next to me randomly asked, "Are you a Christian?"

I thought what a strange question for a stranger to ask, but I said yes. She then said she felt prompted to give me a book. The name of the book was, *Do What Jesus Did.* She didn't understand why she was doing it, and neither did I. However, we struck up a conversation, and I told her some of my healing story. Her eyes widened, and her body stilled. With emotion in her voice, she said, "I understand why I needed to give you this book." The joy on her face made it glow.

I had never heard of this book or the author, but I knew it was something I had to read. I felt the cover as I turned it over to read the back cover, then turned it back to reread the title. There was something special about the book, and I felt compelled to open it right there and begin reading it. As my eyes scanned the words on the page, my heart and mind could feel something, but I could not understand the magnitude of the book until I took it out again later. I discovered that the reason we are all chosen and receive the Holy Spirit is so we can go out and do what Jesus did.

That was the hardest part—to accept and understand everything that had happened to me. However, once I began to study the scriptures, I began to read the miracles and teachings of Jesus. As I was reading and studying this, I began to understand how people were healed from evil, impure spirits. I knew this journey of healing because of the Holy Spirit. I knew that I was going to be okay because it was in the Bible. I was not losing my mind.

Why Not You? God deeply loves and values women. He shows this by giving us compelling stories of healing and redemption in the Bible. If God values women and includes them in so many missions to show His love for His children, how can we ignore that? We are also able to receive the same healing and promises as we read about in the Bible. The women of the Bible are heroes, and now I can bravely say I am too! I was and am Fearlessly Chosen! I am willing to go and share my story with the world.

WHY NOT ALL OF YOU?

In Luke 22, it says:

31 "Simon, Simon, Satan has asked to sift all of you as wheat.

32 "But I have prayed for you, Simon that your faith may not fail. And when you have turned back, strengthen your brothers."

33 "But he replied. 'Lord, I am ready to go with you to prison and to death.'

34 "Jesus answered, 'I tell you, Peter, before the rooster crows today, you will deny three times that you know me.'"

I paid attention to this scripture and learned that Satan has asked to sift all of us as wheat. But God says, "I have prayed for you." As I read this, I felt Jesus talking straight to me.

I started thinking, *did Satan ask Jesus about me like He asked about Simon and asked God about Job?* I've spent a lot of time thinking of what happened to Simon and the fact that Jesus prayed for him. Then Jesus used the name of Peter. It is an interesting pattern. I am not comparing myself with them, but it makes me wonder if Satan goes to Jesus, asking about us, and Jesus starts to pray and moves us to our chosen places. Job and Peter had to go through many trials to find their way just as I did.

Satan was sifting me. When I was being tossed back and forth, I asked *why me* because I felt unworthy to focus on God. However, as I was going through the sifting process, Jesus showed me that I was constantly moving for a few reasons: to shake out the bad, shame, and guilt. I needed to let go of it to become who He created me to be. I was trying to find out why when I should have simply focused on trusting in God and accepting it.

I had to go through the sifting to receive complete healing, like Peter was changed from Simon. He was chosen. I, too, was moved out of the old Stacey and into the new Stacey. I have been restored. I have been lifted up again after passing through that terrible night when I laid at Jesus' feet and longed to be healed and forgiven. I have been saved from hopelessness, brokenness, shame, guilt, and betrayal to a restored, better woman, prepared in a higher sense than before to be a confident warrior for God to help others through a similar trial. This is who I was created to be.

When I was at my weakest, most broken place, lying there on the table, Jesus came to me and filled me with His beautiful, healing light. At that moment in time, I imagined a confused little girl, that shamed woman, and I felt the love, forgiveness, and beauty of Christ Himself. He saw *me* through everything that I had done. He sifted through and pulled out all the good and showed me that I was worthy of His unconditional love and forgiveness. It was at that moment that I knew I was chosen for something bigger than I could imagine. Isaiah 43:10:

"You are my witnesses," declares the Lord,
"and my servant whom I have chosen,
so that you may know and believe me
and understand that I am he.
Before me no god was formed,
nor will there be one after me."

I have cried many tears, lying on the floor looking to Jesus for anything to keep me going, screaming, "Why me? Why did this happen to me?" Now, seven years later, I finally understand. I feel the light now; the sifting is complete, I know *who I am and whose I am.*

The devil is moving on now. He was defeated again. He no longer has control of me because I am a child of God, and it has been through His hands that I have found complete healing. I'm not perfect and will still make mistakes, but Satan does not have the hold on me that he once did. It is my purpose to prepare and WARN others for when the devil comes knocking, and he will.

What I have learned in this journey is that Satan never stops. He never lets up the fight and tries to wear us out and wear us down. But the counterbalance is that Heavenly Father and Jesus and the Spirit NEVER give up on us! Jesus was there for me, and He is most certainly there for you. All you have to do is look up.

Even your mistakes and sins can be recycled into something good and pleasing for the Lord.

There have been many times along the way that I could have given up or given in, but Jesus was always there praying for me to keep getting up and moving forward. The devil has been working hard to have me, but Jesus defeated him at the cross, and my sins are forgiven. The enemy has no power over me. 2 Timothy 2:10 says:

"Therefore I endure everything for the sake of the elect, that they too may obtain the salvation that is in Christ Jesus with eternal glory."

It was all the people in the Bible that saved me. Those stories gave me my story, because without their experiences I could have never stepped out to tell mine, and that is the reason Jesus saved me.

Why not you? God uses the best way to touch each of us because He knows us. He is our Creator, our Protector, and our Father. He knew what I would respond to and what would motivate me to seek Him. I was given a journey to find the truth. He has been eternally patient with me through all the decades I wasted, focused on myself. He never left me but waited until I was ready.

The reason for God choosing you is not in you but in His amazing grace.

"Oh, my child, I see your pain. You have all these questions, asking why this way and why that way? My answer to you is so you can go out and heal the masses. I have planted you exactly where I need you. Many people need healing because of what is inside them, not because of the disease itself. I need you to see, to feel the cause that cannot be evaluated as mainstream medicine sees it, but spiritual healing of your soul.

"The world is changing, needing healing in new ways. I am bringing about miracles that are springing up around you. Throw out the old. Today is a new day, and I am moving in a new direction. You have been given a purpose, but you are still avoiding the truth. I have been with you every step of the way. If we are to defeat the enemy and his roaming in this kingdom, we must get to the source—the people.

"Remember, I led you along the path that most people are avoiding, showing you a new way. Do not lose sight of Me. I freely give these gifts, and I can freely take them back. This journey was specifically made for you. Stop seeking other people's ways. Stepping out in faith with Me is all you have now, but know that I will never leave you nor forsake you."

That was from God to you. I want to leave you with this thought. *Why was I chosen by God for this calling?* Because He is God, and He knows my heart better than I do. He wants to bring to pass my eternal life and salvation. I don't question God now as much as I did before.

When His hands reached out to me as I lay on the table, I saw the marks in his hands. The scars were a reminder that He has already paid the price for all of my wrongdoings. I have been bought with a price. The light that flowed from him filled me, cleansed me, and knew me to the very cells that created me. My physical healing was complete, and my spiritual healing had just started. I knew that I accepted His will and that I will do my best to move the healing work forward.

You don't have to dwell on the question of *why me*, but you can embrace *Why not me?* And why not you? He longs to heal you.

Come, be chosen, follow Him, and live in His Love.

NOTES

Scripture: New International Version

Chapter 3. Nelson, Heather Davis. Un-Ashamed. Crossway. 2016

Chapter 6. Dawkins, Robby. Do What Jesus Did, Chosen Books. 2013

Chapter 10. https://dictionary.cambridge.org/us/dictionary/english/deceive

https://www.interserveusa.org/gods-promise-to-hagar-clearing-up-a-misunderstaning/

A JOURNEY THROUGH HIS HANDS TO COMPLETE HEALING!

Have you ever said any of these things?

- "I don't know how to get over the past."
- "I don't know why everything is always such a drama."
- "I want relief, but it's so hard to talk about what has happened."
- "I'm tired of going to doctors and never getting any answers."
- "I don't want to live with sadness, depression and anxiety all the time."

If you can relate to any of those statements, then after reading *Fearlessly Chosen,* you now know about the ME FIRST process and how it can be life-changing for you!

Before my dramatic healing experience, I thought the feelings of tortured shame and guilt, lack of confidence, and struggle I dealt with daily were my lot in life. I thought I would have to accept it. But it was an attack on my gifts, my calling, and my identity in Christ!

God created us to be healthy in body, soul, and spirit. God is more committed to your healing, joy, and freedom than you are. Do you believe that? God sees you in pain and being tortured by shame, bound by guilt, and feeling as if you deserve to be punished and not forgiven! It hurts Him!

God showed me the way to total transformation is through a process I call, **ME FIRST**! God asks us to have Him first. He is the first ME FIRST. Then we are led to the "**ME FIRST**" path. The results have truly been amazing. I learned:

- How to get over the past.

- How to process drama and traumatic events.

- How to open up and express emotion, pain, and fear to help clear a path to your answers.

- How to get answers even when you have exhausted all known avenues of healing.

- How to find happiness, joy, and peace.

Discovering who I am and whose I am led to a life of transformation in spirit (God), soul (thoughts/emotions/heart), and body. I offer my full story to help you find your transformation too.

Click here www.staceylucascoaching.com/ for your FREE gift to start your healing journey. If you would like more information, email me at stacey@liberatedsoulretreat.com

ABOUT THE AUTHOR

Stacey Lucas is an author, speaker and transformational coach who helps women in chronic emotional and physical pain liberate themselves by healing body, soul and spirit.

Once struggling herself with chronic pain that could not be diagnosed, Stacey experienced the miraculous healing of God in her body and went on a powerful journey with Him to heal her soul and spirit as well. She then found her purpose in helping others do the same thing. Today, Stacey supports women through her Deeper Path and Soul Liberation coaching programs.

With over 20 years' experience as a certified medical assistant in trauma, surgery, family, and pediatric care… Stacey has witnessed first-hand that the healing offered by traditional healthcare is incomplete. She understands through her own experience and that of many other women the need to be healed in spirit and soul, as well.

Stacey has a passion for missions and has served on the field in Africa, were she was baptized in the Indian Ocean— proving that God can take ordinary things and turn them into extraordinary ones! She is also passionate about helping survivors of sex-trafficking and has trained to help women overcome burnout and second-hand trauma.

When she's not helping women heal, Stacey enjoys being a mom to Katey and Jacob, and "Nina" to her beloved grandchildren. She enjoys life in a camper in Kentucky, which she and her husband purchased after God led them to sell their home. While loving her life on the road, Stacey is also president of Soul Liberation.

Lightning Source UK Ltd.
Milton Keynes UK
UKHW020207161020
371670UK00012B/283